THE WHITE SHIRT

THE
WHITE
SHIRT

Find Your Peaceful & Life-giving
Career at Any Stage of Life

MICHAEL ALAN TATE

Includes a Step-by-Step Guide to Design Your
One-Page Career Strategy in One Week

NEW YORK

LONDON • NASHVILLE • MELBOURNE • VANCOUVER

THE WHITE SHIRT

Find Your Peaceful and Life-giving Career at Any Stage in Life

© 2019 Michael Alan Tate

Published in New York, New York, by Morgan James Publishing. Morgan James is a trademark of Morgan James, LLC. www.MorganJamesPublishing.com

The Morgan James Speakers Group can bring authors to your live event. For more information or to book an event visit The Morgan James Speakers Group at www.TheMorganJamesSpeakersGroup.com.

ISBN 9781683508717 paperback
ISBN EB 9781683508724 eBook
Library of Congress Control Number: 2017918434

Cover & Interior Design by:
Christopher Kirk
www.GFSstudio.com

The White Shirt is a work of fiction. Names, characters, places, events, and incidents are the products of the author's imagination or are used fictitiously. Any resemblance to actual persons, living or dead, is entirely coincidental.

Illustrations by Drew Young
Editorial Assistance by Minnie Lamberth

In an effort to support local communities, raise awareness and funds, Morgan James Publishing donates a percentage of all book sales for the life of each book to Habitat for Humanity Peninsula and Greater Williamsburg.

Get involved today! Visit
www.MorganJamesBuilds.com

*You need not see what someone is doing to know
if it is his/her vocation, you have only to watch
their eyes: a cook mixing a sauce, a surgeon
making a primary incision, a clerk completing
a bill of lading, wear the same rapt expression,
forgetting themselves in a function. How
beautiful it is, that eye-on-the-object look.*

—W. H. Auden

*For you created my inmost being;
you knit me together in my mother's womb.
I praise you because I am fearfully and wonderfully made;
Your works are wonderful, I know that full well.*

— Psalm 139:13-14 (NIV)

DEDICATION

This book is dedicated in loving memory of Richard N. Bolles. Dick was a man of intelligent, grace-filled faith. His insights and advice moored my understanding of the science and art of career advising. Of all the things he taught me, three ring always in my ears: One, the true task of the career coach is healing, two, what separates the professionals from the con artist in this work is that the pros can help you create a plan, and three, he would say with a twinkle in his eye, "What works in job search works in life."

Salute, Dick

TABLE OF CONTENTS

PART I
The White Shirt Story

PART II
The White Shirt Strategy Guide

Part I

The White Shirt Story

INTRODUCTION

Crisis to Calling

At thirty years old I was in a career that I believed was my life calling. A mentor had directed me to this vocation with the sincerest intent. With his help, my postgraduate studies were in this field, and here I was—an administrator and educator. I enjoyed being in this role. I was good at my tasks. The organization was growing, even setting new records. I loved the people there. By all outward signs, all was good.

But something was missing.

I loved the work I was doing, but the pressures of the environment were too much for me. I just didn't fit. I began to dread going into the office, and it got worse. Depression set in. I felt trapped. Having dedicated my life (to this point) to the noble work I was doing, how could I even consider getting out now—when I was barely in?

Family and friends were proud of me, and, of course, my pride was on the line as well. But things weren't getting any better. I saw this clearly the day my family and I were driving back from an out-of-state vacation. As we crossed the state line toward home and got closer to my return to my workplace, the migraines started. A few months later I was in the emergency room with boils over most of my body. It was over. A few weeks later I resigned.

Relief.

No more migraines, the boils went away, but now what? I knew what I didn't want to do, but what did I want to do? I knew I needed to change fields, but to what? How?

I tried searching on my own by responding to job-opening ads but with little success. With my educational background, I was astonished that something better wasn't showing up for me. Money was running out, so I finally sought professional help with a career counselor—an expensive professional career counselor. Or, considering the cost, at least I thought I was getting a professional. He turned out to be a lot less.

The counselor gave a few career assessment tests, then declared a career that was a perfect fit for me, and we sent out 500 resumes. That was the plan. He knew it would work. He was wrong.

I had only one response—after 500 resumes to 500 organizations. Five hundred HR people looked at me, and only one said, "OK, let's talk." I had one interview, then no returned call. My discouragement had only gotten worse.

"What is wrong with me?" I asked myself over and over. "I know I have skills, drive, and character to be a great employee. Hadn't I proved myself already? What's the deal?"

But by now I had gotten even more depressed than when I was at my last job. I told the professional career counselor how I felt, and he stopped returning my calls. Exasperated, I cut ties with the counselor, and at that moment I decided, "I will do whatever it takes so no one who needs career help will have to endure what I went through."

My crisis was now my second calling.

Almost broke, I paid my bills through a series of sales jobs as I pursued my new vocational vision. In the meantime, I told a friend what I wanted to do and asked for her advice. She helped me think through a plan and stood by me during my search. She suggested I contact a guy named Phil Ronniger, a career consultant in Louisville, Kentucky.

Phil was a real pro. He mentored me for over a year, which set me on the path to this second calling. I will forever be indebted to him for all he gave me, but the turning point was when he recommended I spend some time with Richard Bolles, the author of *What Color is Your Parachute?* I did. That time with Bolles changed my life forever. His wisdom and insights on career transition strategy helped me finally realize that there was nothing wrong with me when I couldn't find the right job.

The problem was, I chose the wrong strategy.

Simply put, using resumes, applying for job postings, and asking people about job openings was then and still is the worst way to find a good job. A recent article in *Forbes* magazine restated what has been true for the past twenty years, "An incredible 80 percent of available jobs don't get posted."

So even with all the online job listings and internet job search razzmatazz these days, if you rely on this strategy, there are a couple of things you can be sure of: you may find a job that will probably not be a fit and you'll get depressed and sick; or you won't find a job and beat yourself up so much that you'll get depressed and sick.

Choose the healthy path instead.

Research published in the journal *Human Relations* backs up my claims—showing that employees who stay in a job because they feel they don't have other options are more likely to experience burnout and emotional exhaustion. Further, researchers from Australian National University found that those in poor quality jobs were five times more likely to be depressed as those in good quality work. And even if individuals move from being unemployed into poor quality jobs, their mental state may actually experience a greater decline than if they had stayed unemployed!*

Five years after my time with Dick Bolles I had built a successful career transition firm and then sold it to a national consulting firm. After several years of dealing with the big firm bureaucracy, I wanted something different. But I had seen several other managers in my state of mind go to top management and human resources to ask about other internal growth opportunities. None of them had much success. Most left to start their own firms.

Facing a different type of career transition, I thought back to what I had learned. Instead of following that well-worn trail to the HR office, I took the trail less trodden.

I wrote my vision and a plan for the next stage in my career. I shared it with a colleague who, by the way, did not work for our firm. He kept my plan confidential. Three months later, the position that I had envisioned was created, and it was offered to me. I never asked for it.

I cannot explain how this happened, but I do know that history has proven that a person with a vision and plan can change the world.

As a Christian seeking after God's heart, I try to read from the Bible each day. There is a lot in there about the power of planning. A favorite verse of mine is: "The plans of the diligent lead to profit as surely as haste leads to poverty" Proverbs 21:5 (NIV).

There is even more written in the Bible (as well the sacred texts of other religions), about the supernatural favor that flows from prayer and thankfulness. I don't understand it, but I do know when prayer and planning are a consistent part of my life,

I am more thankful, and unexplainable (or supernatural) things happen more often.

Why do I tell these stories about myself? What I learned through my experiences laid the foundation for the pages that follow. So, if you are in a career crisis, whether large or small, this may be the turning point you were hoping for.

Over the last twenty years, I've worked with hundreds of successful executives, entrepreneurs, technical professionals, and clergy (and their college-age kids) who want a simple action-focused plan to effectively manage career transitions. A picture of both the struggles individuals go through as they face unknown career futures and the structure they use to create their plan is contained in my story, *The White Shirt*.

In this book I will explain, in parable format, the best strategy to finding your place in the world of work. It is founded on a few universal truths that work as well today as they did centuries ago.

Fortunately for everyone living today, your career purpose is already woven in you. We only have to step back from the outside voices and know three things: the languages we crave to be around, the things we love to tinker with, and the big question, challenge, or problem that will not let us go until we act on it.

Once this is clear, the answer to "What will I do next?" will be self-evident.

The White Shirt is an imaginative illustration of how a young man discovered and applied a few timeless principles to find his place in the world. In the process, he learned how to design a simple plan to move into a peaceful and prosperous career at any stage in life. These processes and principles make up a planned approach that works as well in reality as it does in this story.

When you finish the story there is guide to a seven-step process (which can be done in a week) to create your career plan. And if you really want to find your ideal career quicker and enjoy the process more, do this with a friend.

Before you get started, please go to the website at whiteshirt-book.com to view a three-minute video about the book and the seven steps. You may also want to have a notebook or journal handy as you read the book to give you a place to record questions and other thoughts that come up.

I am excited for the journey you will be taking. You can turn your crisis into your calling.

Sincerely,

Michael Alan Tate

*Annotations for the research referenced and even more astounding facts about how career fit impacts health, longevity, and overall happiness are found on my website: whiteshirtbook.com

CHAPTER 1

They had been friends since boyhood, and now the four of them were becoming young men. As a matter of fact, this morning they had taken part in an ancient rite of passage: their futures had been decided. This is how it had always been in their culture.

Their parents had actually done this deciding and, as luck would have it, came to the same conclusion. The four young men would be astronomers, a respected and noble profession. Aaron, Bahram, Gage, and Cyrus would soon know of this fateful decision.

The ceremony that was essential to this rite of passage—where futures were decided and announced—took place late in the afternoon. The boys had dressed in their best robes, washed their feet, wiped off their sandals, and headed for the palace. They entered a large courtyard where parents, teenagers, and other family members had gathered. Each took a seat on the stone floor and looked to the specially built platform where announcements would be made.

Cyrus was expecting to hear that he would be an innkeeper since his father, Alborz, had long been in the hotel business. Surely, he, and later his brother and sister, would join him there. But unknown to Cyrus, Alborz had another plan.

Looking back, Alborz appreciated that his own father had chosen well for him when the decision was announced that he would continue the family business of innkeeper. Indeed, Alborz had taken naturally to this path and had invested in inns across the empire. Though he was proud to have done well, his success and masterful abilities meant that he could choose a higher status for his son Cyrus. And what could be higher than the study of the stars?

For Alborz, therefore, the decision was firm: this son would not follow in his footsteps but would raise their family name in a position in the palace as chief astronomer. He stood to the side of the platform, moments away from delivering this good news to his son, and he was ready. According to tradition, future astronomers were given white shirts as part of this public pronouncement. Alborz kept his son's shirt tightly folded and hidden in his robe as he waited for his time to speak.

"Alborz," the king's chancellor finally called. Alborz stepped onto the platform with pride and purpose.

Within the gathering, Cyrus heard Alborz call his name. He stood and nervously tugged on his robe. The walk to his father seemed very long, though it was only a dozen paces. The distance seemed even longer when Cyrus almost tripped as a sandal got caught in a rock. *Did my father see that?* he wondered, embarrassed. Cyrus hoped the stumble had gone undetected, for he knew his father would not be pleased to see a mistake in such a public place. Steadying his balance and trying his best to mimic his father's confident gait, Cyrus stepped onto the ceremonial stage.

He was very curious to hear what his father would say. But Alborz was careful to keep the white shirt hidden and gave no hint of his decision until he made this pronouncement. "Cyrus, my son, I have chosen for you to become an astronomer."

The crowd cheered with approval even as Cyrus recovered from his own surprise. He had heard his father's voice shape his future through the utterance of this unexpected word. Then he saw the white shirt come quickly from out of his father's robe and felt its weight drape around his shoulders.

Now it was known. An astronomer he would be.

Cyrus did not question the decision. Who was he to know of such important matters? But he did reflect on the appropriateness of the choice as the ceremony continued. He wanted to please his father and to represent his family well, yet he was unsure.

Cyrus's mind was put somewhat at ease when he heard what futures lay ahead for his three closest friends. As their own fathers called their names, he heard the same future: astronomer, astronomer, and astronomer.

"Four boyhood friends become four astronomers," he mused to himself. "I can see how this would be a good thing for our village and our families." Indeed, the heavens were aligned, and their roles were ready and waiting.

For all the boys, the news was somewhat of a surprise. Aaron had been working part-time in his father's construction and engineering company, and he thought his dad would want him to take over the business one day. Similarly, Gage had spent the summers working in his father's bookkeeping business. As for Bahram, his dad was in chariot sales, having worked with several companies in the region as opportunities arose. Bahram had not spent much time in his dad's workplaces, but his mother was a seamstress of some renown. Though Bahram knew little of making clothes on his own, he knew very well how to persuade others of the impressive quality and great value of her fine clothes and robes.

Cyrus surmised that all of that was just kid stuff. Now that they were becoming adults, the boys would all pursue a new path and do so together.

But first—they were still boys, after all, and they wanted to take time to play.

They met that night in front of a campfire. Aaron built it before anyone else arrived, and he directed the others on how to keep it burning. "Aaron is so good at making things happen," Cyrus reasoned. "You can put him in charge of anything and know that it will get done—even better than you thought it could. He will make a fine astronomer."

There was Bahram, too. He's the reason Cyrus was persuaded to join them that night. The truth is, Cyrus had tried to beg off from this little gathering. He had wanted to stay home and write his thoughts in his scroll. But Bahram said, "You have to come. It will be fun with all of us there. Without you, it won't be fun at all." Bahram winked as he persisted. "Now, would you ask us to spend this special night having no fun at all?"

"It's a tradition," Gage offered. "We always get together to celebrate big events. It's important to stick to tradition." Then he added, "You must remember we may not have much time together once our studies begin. I have been looking at the schedule, and it will be quite rigorous. We'll have to apply ourselves to get the learning we need."

Cyrus relented and came to enjoy the fire Aaron had built and listen to the stories Bahram told. They studied the stars and imagined the futures that lay ahead. As they compared white shirts, Aaron said, "Through the four of us, we will build a name for our village that will be known from here to the heavens."

Bahram added, "This is such a wonderful night. Our futures will be as our pasts—together, as friends, as brothers, as family."

All the while, Cyrus admired their certainty while he hid his uncertainty.

When the evening was done, Gage put out the fire and said, "We should go home. Tomorrow will be here very soon." As Cyrus left the gathering, he reflected on the enthusiasm that his friends had expressed. At the same time, he sensed the uneasiness growing inside him.

CHAPTER 2

The king was a good man and wise leader, but his overseer, Gaul, was not. Gaul was in charge of all the workers and apprentices in the palace. He was a hard taskmaster with a short temper and controlling mind. He did not like the new astronomers or the young people who came to work in the palace. To his mind, they thought too much of themselves, were hard to manage, and most of all, were not respectful of their elders as he was taught to be. Though others knew Gaul to be a mean and jealous man, the king believed him to be a loyal man, and he trusted him completely.

For Cyrus, staying out of Gaul's way became his main goal. Cyrus tried very hard to fit into the rigorous schedule that was required of him to become an astronomer and counselor to the king. It's not that he disliked the work. He just felt something was missing. He didn't like the structure. He felt he was being squeezed into a place where he should belong, but the fit was uncomfortable.

He did make a new friend, though, and he found some solace talking with her. He'd met Hester in the classrooms and could tell she was brilliant. Organized and efficient, she led the study groups. Her leadership skills were so strong, in fact, even Gaul seemed to like her.

Just recently, Hester had said to him, "Isn't it amazing that we have a chance to study these wonderful subjects and gain such knowledge about our universe? I feel as if I was born to do this work. I am so lucky to be here."

Cyrus had smiled and agreed. What else could he do? Hester's joy also made him wistful. He wondered, *What would it be like to know that you're right where you need to be, pursuing the career that you're meant to pursue?*

Cyrus was intimidated by Hester but also reassured by her wisdom and helpful nature. He almost felt that he could talk to her. But there were some concerns he just couldn't admit to having. Indeed, the uneasiness he had felt on that first night had grown into a discomfort that permeated all he did. Even as he studied, he grew numb. He could feel it. He began to procrastinate in his tasks. He just couldn't bring himself to act on simple things. Whenever he saw Gaul, he always expected—and usually received—criticism that made him feel worse.

The more disconnected Cyrus felt from what he was supposed to be doing, the less he wanted to be around his old friends. Preferring to keep to himself, he stopped spending as much time with Aaron, Bahram, and Gage. But from what he could tell, they were doing well. They were following the course that had been laid out for them and were proceeding through their education and apprenticeship. There was no doubt in his mind that his friends would achieve prominence and importance, and family and friends from home would be proud of their successes.

Feeling alone in his struggle, Cyrus knew he couldn't tell Hester of the plans he was making, and he was uncertain if he should tell Aaron, Bahram, and Gage. He felt a sense of shame that he wasn't going to be the man his father wanted him to be. He felt shame too that others were finding this place of status much easier to claim.

But his heart was clear. Something had to change. Cyrus could see as clearly as the stars in the night sky that he wasn't cut out for being an astronomer.

That evening, Cyrus joined Aaron, Bahram, and Gage at their dinner table. The young men talked amiably about old times, but as they finished their meal, Cyrus couldn't hold in his feelings any longer. Dejected by his failure, he admitted to his friends that he was not happy and wished to leave palace service.

"Not here," Gage cautioned. They all knew better than to speak at the table. Aaron motioned to an official, signaling a request to be excused that was granted with an approving nod. The four young men left the dining room and retreated to a dark corner of the courtyard.

Bahram had held his tongue long enough. "Why leave now?" he asked as he began persuading Cyrus to stay. "You'll get prestige and a lot of gold, and you've got us. You'll be lonely without us, and we'll miss you terribly. Stay, my friend."

Aaron said, "Your place is already decided. There is no need to go off when there is plenty to do and plenty of reward right here. Besides, you'll starve if you leave. Life will be a struggle, and you will be unhappy. This path is a certain one. As an astronomer, you can build a family, and you can build a good treasury for this family. I want you to stay."

Gage weighed in as well. "You've spent many months of study already. If you leave when you're halfway through, you'll lose all the time you spent. You'll have to start over as a lowly apprentice in another place. The path is very clear here. Finish what you've begun."

Cyrus knew his friends meant well, and he thanked them for their encouragement. As they parted, the others were convinced they had talked their friend out of his foolishness. Cyrus, however, held on to the rest of the truth. As he looked ahead to his future, he could not see himself as an astronomer. He would indeed make other plans.

But when? Almost as soon as Cyrus reached his room in the palace, his feelings began to overwhelm him and doubt set in. Sitting on his bed, he began to consider the possibility that he should stay in the program for a few more months until he knew what he wanted to do. Then he could make his move. As he debated with himself, he unbuttoned and removed his white shirt, and held it in his hands. His finger traced the white trim and white ivory buttons as he remembered his father's voice and the touch of his arms coming around him to drape the shirt on his shoulders.

Cyrus thought longingly of his father. Alborz certainly wasn't royalty, yet in some ways the king's confident demeanor reminded Cyrus of his father. He had heard that the king was an understanding leader, and he had wanted to talk with the king about his struggle. Yet when he mentioned this possibility to Gaul a little while back, he was quickly shot down.

"The king is too busy," Gaul had said dismissively. "Get back to your stargazing."

With no one to talk to about what he should do, Cyrus had come to the only conclusion he could: the white shirt just didn't work for him. He was still convinced of this truth. However, his internal debate was dragging him into hesitation. He should sleep on it, he decided. Then the reasoned voice of his father came back to mind.

Cyrus remembered during those days as an early teenager how hard it was for him to get out of bed in the mornings—especially when it was so easy to roll over and sleep for a little longer. Alborz used to scold him especially about this habit of staying in bed till mid-day on the weekend. "You're missing too much of the good part of your life," his father said with dismay. "You won't ever get these years back. Are you going to spend them rolling over, as you say, for just a few more minutes?"

Cyrus had learned a hard lesson on one of those sleepy mornings when he missed his chance to join his friends on an excursion into the neighboring kingdom. Plans had been made for weeks, and when it was time for two large caravans to leave on their journey, the earlier group assumed Cyrus would be coming with the later caravan, while the later group assumed he'd already gone ahead with the first. So, when Cyrus rolled over that one last time and saw through the window the position of the sun in the sky, he felt in the pit of his stomach that he had missed his chance to enjoy something he had planned for a long time. Still, he gave it a shot, jumping out of bed immediately, rushing as fast he could across town. But no luck, the caravans were gone.

Heartsick and back at home, Cyrus sought out his father to sort through his feelings. After all, Alborz would have never had something like this happen to him. "Father, is there something wrong with me?" Cyrus asked with a heavy sigh. "I mean, how do you achieve so much and have the drive to get so much done... when I'm..." Cyrus couldn't finish the statement and meant to let his father fill in the blank with the criticism he deserved. But Alborz, recognizing his son's suffering, took the teaching route.

"You're normal is what you are," Alborz responded. "Many times I don't feel like taking an action even though I know I need to and want to. When this happens, I remember my days as a boy when I would run in the city races, and the official would say 'Ready, Set, Go,' and everyone jumped forward off the starting line. When I'm lying in bed and want to go back to sleep and put off the things I need to do, I say to myself, 'Ready, Set, Go!' And I take an action. I get up. Then when I take that first action, I feel like doing more.

"So now, when great ideas for my business pop into my head, instead of thinking too much about them, I say, 'Ready, Set, Go' and take an action towards that idea. Sometimes the ideas prove to not be so great, but quite a few do, as you see from my success. Many people sit in their homes or at the city gate all day and talk about their grand ideas. They say I am lucky, but I have found the more actions I take, the luckier I get. Mind you, the low achievers aren't lazy. They just allow their feelings to rule their decisions and behaviors, like they have seen most other people do. They have never been taught otherwise. Successful people have decided that life doesn't work that way. Take an action, then feelings follow and lead to more action."

"You make it sound so easy," Cyrus said with admiration but also uncertainty. "I'm just not sure I could do that."

"Well, did you see how fast you moved this morning once you got up?"

"Yeah," Cyrus said wistfully.

"So you know that taking a quick action can be done?"

"Yes, I do."

This conversation replayed in his head as Cyrus's attention returned to his room in the palace. He lay the white shirt aside, then he took a quick breath and said, "Ready, Set, Go." He stood up, pulled on a fresh shirt, grabbed his satchel and began packing his belongings. As he turned to go, he lingered just long enough to stare at the white shirt one last time.

Cyrus knew he could not live up to what the white shirt represented, but he couldn't bear to part with it either—not just yet. He rolled up the shirt and shoved it in his satchel with all the other things he would carry into the unknown. Then, as the hour neared midnight, Cyrus stole quietly through the palace and into the darkened city.

◆ ◆ ◆

Know What
You Don't Want

◆ ◆ ◆

*What tasks are you required to do that
drain your energy?*

*What factors in your environment feel like
an emotional drag or weight?*

CHAPTER 3

The next morning, when word reached the king's chambers that Cyrus had left during the night, the king called for Gaul. "What happened?" he asked the embarrassed and angry overseer.

Gaul's response was rambling—something about "disrespectful, unappreciative children." When he was dismissed from the king's presence, he left in a sulk.

Soon, Gaul's fury rang through the palace hallways: "How dare he!" After all, those who were honored to be chosen to prepare for service to the king, especially in the esteemed role as astronomer, had never been given the option to say, "No, thank you." Once you were given your white shirt, the only acceptable response was obedience.

Gaul dispatched royal guards to find Cyrus. First, they questioned the watchmen in the high towers. Had they seen a boy leave the palace last night? None had. The guards moved on to question those who knew Cyrus best.

Aaron, Bahram, and Gage were sitting in the courtyard discussing where Cyrus could be when they saw the guards quickly approaching. The guard captain pressed hard in his questioning, but the three young men were unable to offer any clues as to where Cyrus may have gone. Finally, the guards turned and left as the captain issued his caution: "For now we find no wrongdoing, but we and Gaul will be watching you to see if you help your friend run from his responsibilities."

When they were alone again, Aaron said, "Cyrus has made a mistake, and he will pay for his mistake. Actions have consequences."

Gage said, "This is terrible. Now that Cyrus has left, that will mean more work for us to do, and what if the work is too hard? Besides, we have been given white shirts for a reason, and he should have stayed and fulfilled his responsibilities."

Bahram said, "What does it matter what we do? The king's decisions are the only ones that matter, and I'm tired of all these studies too. I should have joined Cyrus."

Aaron would hear none of it. "If you did, we wouldn't have anything to do with you, and as it stands, our friendship with Cyrus is over."

Bahram responded, "If that's how you feel, you aren't much of a friend to me or to him." He stormed off.

By this time, Gage had fallen silent. He walked off glumly, leaving Aaron standing alone in the courtyard. For his part, Aaron took a deep breath and exhaled. Then he walked to the astronomers' laboratory and began to straighten and reroll their learning scrolls and place them in the proper order.

CHAPTER 4

Cyrus had walked quietly into that fateful night, deep in thought. He had no illusions that the path ahead would be easy. He knew as well that his father would be very unhappy with his choice. Still, he could not ignore the pull to go by his old home place. He waited in the dark, imagining his parents sleeping soundly—unaware that their son had thrown away the bright future they had so carefully planned.

At the first signs of stirring, he tapped lightly on the door. His mother, Lena, was awake. Though she was clearly surprised and concerned at the sight of her son, she hugged him warmly. "You look thin and hungry," she said. "Let me prepare you a meal."

"I must hurry," Cyrus protested.

"You can hurry after you eat," Lena replied. She prepared a bowl of wheat with honey and almonds and placed it in front of him at the table.

Cyrus was hungrier than he expected. He emptied his bowl and leaned back. As he did, he noticed his mother's writing journal sitting where it always was, on the countertop near her other books. He remembered how she would open it every night at the dinner table and ask each of the children two questions: "What happened today that you are most thankful for? What happened today that are you least thankful for?"

He and his siblings would answer, though they would roll their eyes to each other when their mother wasn't looking—because these questions seemed so adult-like and serious. Then one day Cyrus and his sister asked Lena if she would change the questions to "What was awesome today?" and "What was awful today?" To them, this made the questions more fun, and Lena agreed. Now they looked forward to their thankfulness chat each day.

Lena always made notes about their responses. "It is important to write down things that are important in life," she would say. "One day it might help you or someone else when facing a big decision."

She certainly had helped him make better choices as a child, he remembered. *Maybe she can help me now*, he thought.

As Cyrus had grown older, Lena had attempted to instill in him this daily habit of writing his thoughts and ideas. He tried from time to time, and he thought about making notes when big things happened, but he never stuck with it. Now he wished he had.

He was shaken from his moment of fond memories and regrets when heard the telltale signs of Alborz moving toward the kitchen. His father's feet were heavy but stopped suddenly. Clearly, Alborz had seen Cyrus at the table. In a tone that was both curious and cautious, Alborz asked, "What is this? Do future astronomers get breaks from their studies?"

"Father," Cyrus said as he looked up, "I left the palace."

Alborz held up his hand, for he knew from Cyrus's countenance that whatever words followed could not mask what this meant. From a heart more broken than angry, Alborz said, "This is a disgrace. You must leave now. The king will not be happy with you or me, and I don't want to know anything that I will be pressured to tell Gaul or his guard, for they will surely follow you here." Without another word, Alborz walked into the morning light, steeled for the day's work and for the fallout to come.

Cyrus choked back emotion as he slowly stood. "He is right, Mother. I should have known. I must leave. The palace will come looking for me, and they will start here." Cyrus could barely stifle a sob as he said, "I shouldn't have caused you this shame and embarrassment."

His mother pulled him close. "You must go, but our hearts will go with you. Of that you can be sure. Find your way, son, and we will see you again."

Cyrus released from his mother's hug. He picked up his satchel and started to turn. "Wait," he said. Opening his satchel, he pulled out the white shirt. "Take it away from me, please. I don't deserve it. And you and Father deserved better than what I did."

Lena touched the cloth gingerly. "Your father wanted the best for you when he picked your white shirt."

"I know he did, but ..." Cyrus began.

Lena stopped him from saying more.

"Son," she continued, "he still wants the best for you. Take the white shirt with you wherever you go, and though you may never be an astronomer, let the shirt itself be a reminder of the love that is always with you. And know that I will pray for you every day."

As he turned with shirt in hand, Lena handed him a small goatskin bag. "Take this too," she said. "In this bag you'll find hard bread, parched corn, raisins, and figs to help you get strong again, and a journal for writing." He peered into the bag, looking at the journal, wondering if he would use it now.

Lena continued, "I have told you this before, but let me remind you again. I have found that if I am discouraged, writing one thing I am thankful for and one thing I am not thankful for each day lifts my spirits. Take a moment to record both positive and negative observations." Then she smiled, adding, "Or, as you say, 'awesome and awful.' Writing this and your other ideas in your journal may help you as you search for your place in the world."

Cyrus reached for one quick hug. Then, with bag in hand and the white shirt returned to his satchel, he left his home and began a long walk that he continued for several days and nights to put some distance between him and his pursuers. He was near exhaustion when saw a small trail off the main road and followed it to the foot of the mountain. He came upon an empty cave near a brook of fresh water. He moved in to rest, to stay out of view of any palace guards, and to think about his life.

Lena's thoughts were on her son as well. She had wondered about going to see the king, whom she had met with Alborz a few years ago. Surely she could tell him about her son and work this out. But she knew her idea would go no further. Alborz would never allow it, and that busybody Gaul, who screened all the king's visitors, would never let her near the palace.

Lena prayed for her son every day.

◆ ◆ ◆

Take a Bold Step

◆ ◆ ◆

*Have you ever had a strong urge or instinct
to do something bold and you act on it?
What did you learn?*

CHAPTER 5

Cyrus had been living in his cave for some days now. Clearly, his new abode was not nearly as comfortable as his palace quarters, but he was starting to feel somewhat at home. Still, he was hungry. He had eaten the last of the figs and bread his mother had provided, and he knew he couldn't go back to the nearest village he passed for fear of being seen.

He remembered, though, that Lena had given him more than food as she said good-bye. She had promised to pray for him every day, and Cyrus had no doubt that she was doing so. Her strong faith had always helped her find her way and was a blessing to their family.

So, Cyrus began to pray too. He prayed as Lena had taught him, expressing gratitude and asking God for food for this day.

He sat and waited. Noon came and then the evening. No food dropped from heaven.

He ventured outside, hoping to search for something to eat. He had no luck. Even though there were lots of quail, doves, and hares that lived on the mountain, they were too fast to catch. He found some wild radishes and onions, but what kind of meal is that without fish, meat, or grain?

Frustrated and famished, Cyrus returned to the cave and built a fire. At least he had light and warmth, but he couldn't settle down. Restless from hunger, he walked farther back in the cave to see what might be there. He took an unexpected step, stumbling on a large rock. He fell on his hands and knees.

Discouragement was setting in. He thought to himself that he had for a time lived in the palace. Now here he was on his hands and knees in a remote cave. With great weariness, he started to push himself up. As he moved his hand into a better position, he felt something round in the soft dirt.

Cyrus dug down a few inches and began to pull out his discovery. He had stumbled upon a clay jug. As he finished digging out the jug, his fire gave enough light that he could see the jug was laying next to a cooking pot with a lid.

"Someone has been this way before," he said to himself. "Some other traveler who planned to come back this way probably stored these here for his return."

When Cyrus lifted the lid on the cooking pot, he discovered a handful of wheat left in the bottom. He was quickly outside the cave again, gathering water from the stream. And that night, he cooked some of the wheat in the pot. Afterwards, he washed the pot clean and turned it over to dry. Then he noticed the mark on the bottom, a mark of the craftsman. He thought he had seen it before on some of the pottery in the palace, but he was tired and gave it no more thought.

With food in his belly, Cyrus lay down to sleep thinking of the luck of his find. Then he remembered his mother's advice about thankfulness. Cyrus picked up his journal and wrote "finding a jug, pot, and wheat." That's when he noticed a note his mother had written in the journal. Tears filled his eyes as he read her words and imagined hearing them in her own voice. Comforted, he slept well.

My dear son,

When you were very small, I couldn't help but notice how perceptive and insightful you were with people. As I watched you immersed in play, you always seemed to be drawn to inventing a new or better way to do a game or add something creative to your project that day, and you are naturally gifted at this—better than you realized then or now.

You were never good with lots of rules or hurried days. Much different from your brother and sister, who loved to be with groups of friends all the time, you were most happy when you were alone or with your one best friend—with room to be yourself and a variety of things to do during your long days playing outside. As you seek your place in the world, please remember who you are and your special talents, and that God's voice is easier to hear in the silence of nature.

All my love,
Mother

The next morning, Cyrus read the note again. Then he turned the page and wrote down some of the things he did not like about the work as an astronomer at the palace. Then he wrote the things he enjoyed there. He realized that he was doing the "I'm most thankful for and least thankful for" exercise his mother had modeled. He felt much better for having done this simple task. He said to himself, "This will be my habit from this day on."

Cyrus stoked the fire and prepared the last bit of wheat, then went on a search for more food. With restored confidence, his search yielded better results. He found a few grapes that grew on the mountain and dug some edible roots near the brook. He knew that it took more than vegetation to regain his strength, so he designed some bird traps from vines and sticks and set them out each morning before sunrise. He even set a fish trap in the stream. Almost every day thereafter, he caught a quail or dove and occasionally a small fish. He seasoned them with his onions and radishes, and after several good meals, he was gaining his physical strength back.

Sitting in the cave entrance in the late afternoon, watching the sun's rays melt into the trees on the hillside, Cyrus experienced a sense of awe, a feeling that he was beginning to find himself again. His mind flashed back to the king's noisy, busy palace, and he realized how much he had missed and needed nature in his life. He opened his journal and wrote "the wonder of God's nature" on his awesome list.

◆ ◆ ◆

Acknowledge Your Original Design

◆ ◆ ◆

If you were writing yourself a note about what you observe as your best skills, talents, and traits (that no one but you will ever read), what would you write in that note?

CHAPTER 6

One afternoon, Cyrus was at the mouth of the cave stirring a new pot of quail stew when a man about his father's age came walking by.

"Hello," the man said.

"Hello," Cyrus responded.

"It's warm out today, and I am tired from my long walk. Do you mind if I rest here for a while?"

"Certainly," Cyrus said. "I have a jug of fresh water inside. Let me pour you a cup."

"I'm most appreciative, son. My name is Baback."

"Pleased to meet you, sir. My name is Cyrus."

"What brings you to this place, Cyrus?" Baback asked as he stepped through the cave's entrance. "Out of all the places in this great empire, why are you living in a cave right now?"

"Well, it's a long story," Cyrus said. He knew he shouldn't tell anyone of the king's disappointment and Gaul's displeasure—especially when his whereabouts could quickly be reported. But after they talked for a while, this man seemed to be of good character, and he felt he could trust him. Besides, Cyrus was lonely and wanted to talk.

"I left palace service," he admitted. "I don't think the king is very happy with me right now, and I know his overseer, Gaul, is irate. I'll be pressured to go back—or worse—if Gaul or his men find me, so I'm staying out of sight until I can figure out what to do next."

"I see," Baback replied. "That is certainly a predicament."

"And my family…" Cyrus surprised himself when he said out loud what was on his heart. "I had to leave them. I know I've disappointed them. They wanted what was best for me."

"That is a very familiar struggle," Baback said. "I have children who will soon be seeking their vocation, and I had to go through that myself when I was younger. Tell me about the kind of work your family has done."

"Well, my father is a great businessman. He is an innkeeper and has done very well. My grandfather started this business, and my father continued it and grew it into many locations. We're all proud of my father's success. He is an admirable man."

"Pardon me, son. Do you mind if I write on this smooth wall of your cave? I like to see things written out. It helps me think."

"Of course not," Cyrus said, surprised.

Baback found a piece of old hard charcoal near the fire and drew something that looked like a tree on the cave wall. "Your father is an innkeeper… let's write that down." He scratched out the word "innkeeper."

Baback turned back to Cyrus. "Now, what have others done?" he asked.

"One of my uncles went in another direction," Cyrus said. "He is in sales. At first this frustrated my father to no end. He just thought it was words, words, words, and he would say, 'How can you sell something if you don't build anything?'"

Cyrus smiled at the memory of his uncle Naveed. "But my uncle is a fun person to be around. He greets every situation as if it is good news. He and my father were distant for a while, but my father grew to respect Naveed when he saw how many people Naveed could persuade to do just as he wanted."

"Then I will write 'sales' on the wall," Baback said as he began to scratch out more letters.

Cyrus continued, "With Naveed it wasn't the sale for the sale's sake." He paused as he tried to articulate a distinction that he was just now recognizing. "Naveed helped people make decisions that were in their best interest. In other words, if he knew something wasn't right for the person, he would steer them away from that choice. But if he sensed that a product would make a real difference in that person's life or work, he couldn't be stopped until he had made the right case."

"I see," Baback said. "It's interesting that you noticed that. And on your mother's side?"

"Her father was a merchant in Babylon, and her brother and sister joined him in that business. They're very business-minded. I admire how well they've done."

"Merchants," Baback said as he wrote again. "And your mother? Tell me about her."

"Oh, what a wonderful woman. She works with my father at the inns. They share the responsibility for the business—each from their own strengths. The thing I notice about her is that she has an uncanny sense of understanding a guest's real need. What I mean is if they ask for a place to sleep, she knows they need food. Or they'll ask for a cup of water, and she knows they need a place to bathe. She looks past the initial request to what they really need."

Baback looked thoughtful for a moment. "Hmm. I am tempted to call this 'hospitality,' but there must be a better name for one in business who helps the individuals get what they need to perform their tasks." Baback left his original idea on the wall; he made a few more marks and then turned back to Cyrus. "Looks like you come from a fascinating family."

"I do." Cyrus nodded as he studied at the markings on the wall.

"You must have some interesting friends too."

Cyrus smiled weakly. "I do. They're probably mad at me too. We were all given white shirts—Aaron, Bahram, Gage, and I— and we were supposed to do this together. But I left."

"You wanted to stay because your friends were there."

"Yes, that was really the reason—well, it was what my father wanted, and it was what my friends were doing."

Baback nodded. "Those are pretty strong reasons. On second thought, let me change that word. Other people are not the *reason* we make choices. They *influence* why we do what we do. We make the choice of how much influence they have. Does that idea make sense to you?"

Cyrus reflected on Baback's words. "Yes, it does."

"Before I go, let me ask you one more thing."

"Please do," Cyrus said.

"Has anyone in your family worked in a synagogue or temple or a school?"

Cyrus was surprised by the question and gave thought to his answer. Then he shook his head. "Besides my brief time in the king's palace with my friends, I can't think of anyone." He paused for a moment's reflection. "This may not count, but as a matter of custom, all families in my community are required to serve each year in certain religious ceremonies." He went on, "My brother hated the formality, but my sister and I really enjoyed serving in those ceremonies with my father."

"A positive experience in public service then, if not quite a career. There is often a first doctor, first teacher, first something in the family. But you'd be surprised how exposure to types of careers prepares us for our own. It can be very subtle, but it's also very real. As you think about your future, consider the people that influence your life—and what they've done in their own work and lives. Then decide how much influence their choices will have or not have on what you will do with your life. Be sure your decision fits who you are and not who they are."

"I will. Thank you."

"Good luck to you, son." Baback tossed the bit of charcoal into the fire and dusted off his hands. "I've got a little farther to go, and I must make haste while the light is still shining." Cyrus watched as he walked away.

◆◆◆

Parents, Peers, and the Past Matter

◆◆◆

What are the most interesting careers or vocations of your family and close friends? How has exposure to these careers impacted your career choices?

CHAPTER 7

Before he went to bed, Cyrus made a note in his journal about Baback. In his sleep that night, his mind kept going over again and again the influences of his family and friends. He got up a few times and jotted other thoughts and ideas on the wall. The next morning, as he stepped from the cave into the bright sun, he felt surprisingly refreshed after a restless night. Then he heard a cheery greeting from a passerby.

"Hello!"

"Hello, indeed." Cyrus nodded to the gentleman who looked only slightly older than he was himself.

The gleeful man held out his arms as if beholding the day. "It is a beautiful morning, is it not? And so full of opportunity!"

Cyrus smiled uncertainly.

The gentleman turned his head to the side and asked teasingly, "Are you not ready for all the opportunity this day offers, my friend?"

Cyrus shook his head good-naturedly. "I guess I just don't see it as clearly as you do."

"Ah," the gentleman said. "Then let me tell you what I know." He moved closer. "My name is Shadan. And you are?"

"Cyrus."

"Cyrus, my friend, I am on my way to Jerusalem where I will offer one lucky fellow the chance to be part of an incredible opportunity."

"Really?"

"Yes, the city is growing by leaps and bounds, and there will be many travelers coming through very soon, and they'll all have coins in their pockets for purchasing my goods. All I need to do is get a few others to help me get the start-up money to buy a stake in this promise—and business will be booming."

"What is this business that you will be pursuing?" Cyrus asked.

"I will be selling expensive jewelry." Shadan turned his head to the other side. "Now, I shouldn't be telling you this, but you look like you have an honest face. Confidentially, Cyrus, I have found a source not too far from here who is guaranteeing me lowest prices on the finest gems that I can sell for much higher prices to high-paid palace officials to purchase for their wives and even for themselves. Essentially, I'll be turning a small investment into a big payoff for very little effort on my part."

"What if they don't want to buy them?" Cyrus asked.

Shadan waved his hand dismissively. "Not a problem. I will convince them of their need."

Cyrus furrowed his eyebrows as he gave thought to Shadan's words.

"Let me interrupt your thoughts, Cyrus, as I explain a simple mathematical equation. I sell jewelry for ten times the price I pay for the jewelry. The moneyed class—royal officials, successful merchants, landowners, and other well-paid professionals—will be proud to have this kind of magnificence for all to see. They'll be impressed with their own prestige, as will their peers, and the common people will swoon at their gifts." Then Shadan added, "We will be the most famous jewelry dealers in the land. Our fame will spread until people will beg us to let them buy our one-of-a-kind rings, necklaces, and bracelets."

Cyrus nodded as he started to see the possibilities more clearly and got caught up in this big dream.

"The problem is…" Shadan laughed. "Obviously, there has to be a stumbling block or every person in town would be in on this kind of business venture. The problem is I need the cash to pay my jewelry maker, so I can get the goods that I will in turn mark up and resell for a tenfold profit."

"Yes, that is definitely an issue," Cyrus agreed.

"Have you any means, Cyrus, that would allow you to join this incredible opportunity?"

Cyrus shook his head. "I have no money."

"If not money, anything at all worth selling?"

Cyrus took a breath and exhaled as he considered his resources. "Nothing… well… oh, I don't know."

"There was hesitation. You do have something?" Shadan prompted.

"Not really. I was just thinking the only thing that I have that I could even think about selling is a white shirt."

Shadan stepped closer. "The kind the astronomers are given?"

"Actually, yes."

"Do let me see it, Cyrus. You'd be surprised how valuable a royal white shirt can be on the black market… or rather, what I meant to say is, how valuable they are to royalty in other kingdoms."

"Really?" Cyrus asked.

"Really. Let me see it."

Cyrus stepped back into the cave. As he located and opened his satchel, he reached in to touch that white shirt. Lifting it out, he heard his father's voice and felt the touch of the cloth on his shoulder, even as he heard his mother's words describe the love that he carried with him. He stopped, unable to take the shirt out into the light to show Shadan. He placed it back in his satchel.

As he returned to Shadan, he said, "I'm sorry. I misled you. I do have a white shirt, but I cannot sell it. Thank you for offering me this opportunity, but I will look for another."

Shadan responded, "I'm sorry too, Cyrus. I wish you good fortune, even as I look to welcome another lucky soul into my profitable enterprise. You still might consider Jerusalem or the city nearby. With the crowds they are expecting, a lot of businesses will be hiring clever people like you."

"Thank you. I will keep that in mind," Cyrus said.

CHAPTER 8

The day turned out to be a long one as Cyrus went back and forth on how he had responded to Shadan's offer to get involved in his business venture. Shouldn't he have taken this opportunity when it practically fell in his lap? Was anything that promised more profit going to come along? Where was his "Ready, Set, Go" when he needed it?

Or should he have done as he did—listened to that inner voice that said, "This is not for you." Come to think of it, that's what he had done when he left the palace. Why tie himself so quickly to another option that also wasn't right?

The sun was yielding the long afternoon shadows when another man—an older one—came walking by. Cyrus spoke first. "Hello."

The man looked toward the cave's opening to see Cyrus sitting on a rock. "Hello, young man. It is nice to hear a friendly voice this afternoon."

"May I offer you some water? And a little rest?"

"Thank you kindly," the older man said. "I would appreciate the drink, the time to catch my breath, and a few moments out of the sun."

"Come into the cave then," Cyrus offered. "It's cool inside, and you may rest your feet and quench your thirst."

"Thank you, young man. My name is Darrius. And yours?"

"Cyrus."

"Pleased to make your acquaintance, Cyrus," Darrius said as he walked through the cave's entrance.

Cyrus followed. "Sit on my blanket, please. It's a little more comfortable than the floor."

Darrius eased down as Cyrus poured a cup of water from his jug and handed it to his guest. As the older man sipped, he looked to the younger man offering him this gracious hospitality. "It seems you have something heavy on your mind today. Care to lighten your load by telling me what it is?"

Cyrus sat, crossed his legs, and admitted his concerns. "I have been struggling with some decisions about my career," Cyrus said. "A man came by a day ago, and we talked about my family and my friends and how people influence what you decide to do."

"Does that have anything to do with these markings on the wall?" Darrius asked.

"Yes. He asked me to tell him about the careers that people in my family have pursued."

"Ah, I see."

"Then this other man came by and offered a path to quick profits. I was tempted to follow his plan, but something inside me hesitated. I just couldn't make the decision to go with him."

"I understand," Darrius said. "There is a secret to finding work mission, which leads to career peace, as I call it, that many people never discover. If you think it's going to be profits or fame, you'll be very surprised when you find out it's not. Profit is the easiest to focus on and get approval for, but money for money's sake leaves most people feeling surprisingly empty and wanting more. No matter how much money you gain or fame you receive, there is never enough to give you peace."

"Well, what is this secret?" Cyrus asked. "Tell me your secret so that I'll know what to do and where to go."

"Oh, it's not my secret you want," Darrius replied. "The secret is different for each person. And it's not so much a secret as it is taking time to understand what is most important to you."

"Really?"

Darrius continued, "First, you have a mission for being here—for being here on this earth and in the work you will do. I believe it was designed in you before your birth. Connecting with your design will guide your decision-making. And when you are guided by your reason for being, you make better decisions that lead to a peaceful career."

"My mission," Cyrus mused. "You know, I couldn't have put my finger on it, but when Shadan was talking about quick profits, I felt conflict, not peace for sure. I wanted money, certainly, but I didn't want to get it selling jewelry at a quick, questionable profit. Plus, I wanted respect, but not as an astronomer."

"An astronomer?"

Cyrus was startled by his admission. "That's what my father wanted for me."

"Oh, indeed. I suspect we come from different backgrounds, young man. I can assure you, however, we have something in common. Families, friends—these influences are important to all of us and sometimes lead to our work mission or vocation. And profit is important too. It's not often that someone chooses a career path that won't provide the provisions that are needed in this world. But that's where your mission comes into play. It is like your north star. It stays in the same place and reminds you what is important to you, so you don't get off your path or get lost."

Darrius continued, "This mission draws on a combination of elements—your background and family, your natural interests, talents, and work values. Knowing these factors helps you make better decisions as you consider your family influences and as you evaluate your opportunities for profit.

"Let me show you." He picked up the charcoal and drew on the wall. "A career is like wearing a hat and standing in a field. The field represents the type of business or organization you would work in, and the hat represents your job title. For example, a person could wear the hat of sales in the field of real estate, fine jewelry, or inn keeping. Another person could wear the hat of bookkeeper, manager, or scientist in the same three fields or others.

"A person's interests help him find his field or type of general industry. Talents and skills indicate the hat you might wear in that field. Values help refine your focus even more by explaining the type of atmosphere that inspires or motivates you to do your best work. See how that works?"

"The drawing helps. I think I understand," Cyrus said.

"I am glad to hear it, young man." Darrius drained the water from his cup. He handed the cup back to Cyrus then picked up the charcoal again. "Let me add one more thing to this drawing." He wrote, "Interests are the languages or subjects you love to be around." Darrius turned back to Cyrus. "Your ears are a very true guide to finding the work that is calling you."

As Darrius handed the charcoal to Cyrus, he said, "I thank you for the rest and the drink. I must keep moving to make it home before nightfall. I have some duties to tend to in the morning."

"You stay busy... at your age?" Cyrus awkwardly asked.

Darrius laughed. "Even though I have all the gold I will ever need to live a good life and support my family, I still have work I enjoy doing." Then he winked and added, "Even when you are old like me, it still feels good to receive a coin or two for some work well done."

"Thank you, sir, for stopping by," Cyrus said as he rose. He wanted more than anything to keep this conversation going, but he hesitated. Surely this kind gentleman had more important things to do than to talk with him. But on impulse, he said to himself, "Ready, Set, Go" and took his chance. "Would you stay for the night and allow me to walk with you toward your home in the morning?" he blurted out. "I would like to learn more about how to find my place, my work mission, and a peaceful career."

Darrius smiled. "I would be pleased to be a guide in your learning. I'll stay, and we'll go together."

Darrius and Cyrus sat by the fire until dusk became darkness. They talked and laughed about their adventures and spoke humorously and wistfully about their families. When stars filled the sky, Darrius laid out his bedroll and was soon off to a peaceful sleep. Cyrus was restless with excitement, but he took the cue of the older gentleman and lay down for the night.

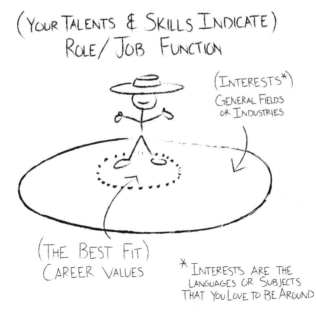

(YOUR TALENTS & SKILLS INDICATE)
ROLE / JOB FUNCTION

(INTERESTS*)
GENERAL FIELDS
OR INDUSTRIES

(THE BEST FIT)
CAREER VALUES

* INTERESTS ARE THE
LANGUAGES OR SUBJECTS
THAT YOU LOVE TO BE AROUND

◆ ◆ ◆

See Your Invisible Skills

◆ ◆ ◆

Have you noticed that it is easier to see what other people are good at than to see what you are good at?

What skills and abilities have others said they see in you?

CHAPTER 9

Before the sun was up, Cyrus awoke and stoked the fire, creating enough light to make out the markings on the cave wall. Reaching for his satchel, he pulled out his journal and wrote down all the writings on the wall.

As Cyrus closed the small book, Darrius stirred. Cyrus offered his guest some breakfast, and as they ate, they shared the wonder of a new sunrise together.

"Thank you. This is the beginning I needed for the journey ahead," Darrius said. Seeing the journal Cyrus had laid aside, he asked, "What have you been recording?"

"I didn't want to forget what I had learned in this cave," Cyrus said as he opened the book to show what he'd just entered, "so I wrote down all those notes from the wall."

"Ah, yes. A good idea," Darrius responded.

"My mother… she gave me some good advice before I left home. She told me to write down each night something that I was thankful for and to make note of other things to help me find my answer."

Darrius grinned when he saw where Cyrus had written "Awesome and Awful" above his lists. Then he said, "When I retired from my business and was struggling with what to do with myself, my wife recommended I start this same daily habit. After about two weeks of recording each day, we sat at our kitchen table and looked at my two lists, and she said, 'There's your answer.' Of course I didn't see it, but Bina explained, 'all you have to do is add more of the things on your thankful list to your life and remove all or most of the things on your least thankful list, and you are on your way to finding your place again.'"

Darrius went on, "I don't remember what I said that day, but today I would say 'awesome.' Both the women in our lives are great teachers."

Darrius stood. "Now, let us go if we're going." And the two men began to walk down the path together.

They had gone a short distance when Cyrus suddenly remembered he had left the jug and cooking pot out and had not returned them to the place in the back of the cave where he found them. He could hear his mother's voice telling him, "Put things back where they belong."

"I am sorry, Darrius, but I must go back to the cave. I forgot something." The older man seemed a bit irritated, but Cyrus explained his need to return the pieces to their place. He ran back quickly and soon returned to find Darrius sitting by the road with a pleased look on his face.

Now their journey began in earnest. For the next few hours, they talked and walked, though it was mostly Cyrus telling about his background in his short life. Darrius kept asking questions but never mentioned much about himself.

As time passed, Cyrus wondered when they would begin working on his career strategy. As lunchtime neared, he realized he didn't even know where they were headed. Finally, he asked, "Where are we going?"

"Bethlehem," Darrius said. "I wasn't born there, as my name might imply to you, but I live in that city now."

"Will we pass through Jerusalem on the way?"

"Yes, we will," said Darrius.

"That is good because I understand there are many opportunities for great jobs there."

Darrius nodded and looked deeply at Cyrus. "But the question is, what kind of job do you want?"

Cyrus answered honestly. "I don't know."

"Let's rest for a moment," Darrius said as he took a seat on a comfortable rock along the path. Cyrus took a nearby rock for his own seat.

Darrius began, "Most people take what comes along or let someone else make their decisions for them. I call that 'working by default.' A few people take time to reflect about what job fits their talents and can explain their skills to others so that finding the right job is easier. Like the drawing I made in the cave. They work by design. Without a good idea of what you want for your next job, you may find yourself back in that cave again. You need to decide if you want a default career or a designed career."

Cyrus answered without hesitation. "I want a design. Where do I begin?"

"First let me show you the plan I designed for myself," Darrius said. He pulled out a journal of his own from his satchel.

Cyrus was surprised that a man who had retired would have a need for a plan, but he kept silent.

Darrius continued, "I haven't looked at this in a while, but I developed this strategy, or as I call it, my repurpose plan, after I turned my pottery business over to my grown children about five years ago. I recognized that they needed to run it on their own without the old man looking over their shoulder. So, I walked away completely—thinking I had plenty of projects at home along with community service activities to keep me busy, and I could spend more time with my lovely wife.

"After a few moons passed, I was bored. My wife, Bina, was frustrated with having me around the house getting in the way of her routine. But it was more than that; I needed some reason to get up every day. I needed a purpose again. I had seen a few of my friends leave the business 'to relax and take it easy,' they said. But they had nothing to do. Most of them got weak, sick, and most died within a few years.

"Bina suggested that I talk with a friend of mine who was in the same 'ship with a sail but without a rudder' state as I was in. We met a few times to talk about what each of us would like to do and how to find a way to have more structure and purpose in our lives. We had a hard time getting much done; you know how old guys tell old stories too much and way too long. We kept getting off track until one day my friend showed me a drawing he had made. He called it his 'work and hobbies chart.'

"His chart had two lists. One list ran down the left-hand side of a page, where he listed all the job titles he had held in his life. Across the top he listed all the fields or types of places he had worked, as well as his hobbies. He had worked as carpenter, a blacksmith, and store manager. His fields were construction, metal works, and retail.

"My friend had always loved and tinkered with knives, so he turned his knife-making hobby into a thriving back-of-the-house retail business. He makes a few amazing, beautiful, and sturdy knives every year. The demand is so high that he can work at his own pace and sell them for as much as he wants. He is a happy craftsman, and his wife is happy too."

Darrius reached into his bag and pulled out a paper. He said, "I did a 'work and hobbies chart' for myself. It was so helpful I keep it with me."

DARRIUS WORK HISTORY & HOBBIES

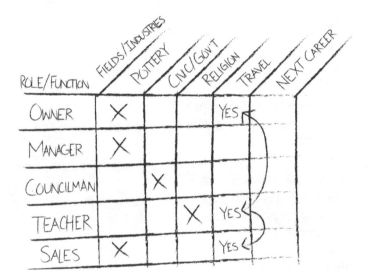

ROLE/FUNCTION	FIELDS/INDUSTRIES	POTTERY	CIVIC/GOV'T	RELIGION	TRAVEL	NEXT CAREER
OWNER	X			YES		
MANAGER	X					
COUNCILMAN		X				
TEACHER			X	YES		
SALES	X			YES		

He continued, "What I ultimately decided was to combine my love for travel, sales, and teaching to be a part-time salesman for my daughter and my son. They want to expand their business to other areas, so I go out and find merchants or other large customers who want our standard pottery or want something custom designed. Then I arrange delivery transportation. I also make my rounds to check on quality and service, as you see on my plan. It is fun, and I don't get in their way. I was coming from such a trip when you so graciously welcomed me into the cave, where I used some of my teaching skills. You can see how all of this fits together in my plan."

Darrius
Repurpose My Work Plan

Background and Current Situation:

Founder and operator of pottery business—twenty-five years

City councilman for ten years

Volunteer teacher of history to young people at synagogue

Seeking to work part-time in sales or customer service

Skills, Interests, and Work Values:

Use my skills in customer service, selling business to business

Apply my knowledge of pottery design and how to deal with affluent clients

Work in place where there are clear goals, incentives for meeting goals, and opportunities to travel and meet new people

Places that fit my goals:

Live near Bethlehem

High-quality craft product business that wants to expand customer base

Retail shop with custom products to sell to affluent customers

School that needs teacher or tutor—to help mold young minds to reach their potential

How you can help me:

Review my plan and advise me on my approach

Suggest names of places or businesses that fit goals

Recommend other people I should talk to about my plan

"I should mention, those who know you well can be import-ant in the development of your plan. My wife had lots of great ideas. She wrote down things she had observed about me, like what I enjoyed doing, the places I was happiest, and, of course, she pointed out what I am not good at, even if I thought I was." Darrius laughed as he thought of his lovely partner in life. "Bina was the one who added the 'how can you help me' part to my plan and suggested the best way to talk about my plan with people. But I am getting ahead of myself. You'll meet Bina soon. Now back to the plan."

Darrius continued, "I don't intend for you to copy this, but most people have never seen a career strategy, and it is easier for some people if they see a model and can see where to start and have a structure of how to proceed. This is an outline that has worked for me and for many others, but you will create yours to fit you… much like how you created the clever traps to catch your supper at the cave or quickly summarized the writing on the cave wall in your journal this morning. So let's get started."

Cyrus felt excitement but also concern. He asked, "Do we have enough time on this short journey to create something this important?"

"For most people, I would answer no, but for you I think it can be done," Darrius replied. "The reason I say this is because I have found that there are two characteristics a person needs to develop so that he or she can find a peaceful career and design a plan to get there. Gratitude is first, and generosity is second. You have displayed these abundantly since I first met you."

Cyrus was humbled by this compliment from such a wise man.

"We have this afternoon and tomorrow morning before we reach my home. You can have your plan by then, if you want it," Darrius explained.

Cyrus immediately replied, "I do."

"I will help you. Now open your journal and write *Talents, Places,* and *People* on one page."

Cyrus did as instructed. Then the men took a drink of water from a goatskin canteen and returned to their walk. Along the way, Darrius shared the skills that he had noticed in Cyrus since they had been together.

Cyrus listened as he fine-tuned the art of writing while walking. He wrote down all the skills and talents Darrius noted. When words fell silent, he looked back over the list, scratched out a few, and adjusted some to fit the way he thought and spoke. By nightfall, Cyrus had several ideas written in his journal.

TALENTS

- PLANNING
- WRITING
- DESIGN
- CONNECTING PEOPLE

PEOPLE

- YOUNG ADULTS
- NOT MIDDLE AGE
- EDUCATED
- NO CHILDREN

PLACES

- CREATIVE SPACE
- FREEDOM
- SLOWER PACE
- TIME TO THINK

Cyrus turned back in his journal and reread the note his mother had written at the front. He was surprised by how closely aligned the things his mother had observed about him as a very young child were to what his new friend saw in him today.

The travelers stopped at the outskirts of Jerusalem to rest near an old public well and to make camp nearby. They built a fire and finished a dinner of hard bread and dates. As they ate, Cyrus said to Darrius, "I appreciate the time you're taking with me to share your wisdom. I believe it will help me find my place."

"Ah," Darrius said. "That brings up an important point. I know your mind is working through all these issues we've been discussing. Before we rest for the night, I'd like to offer one more thought for perspective. There are three questions that everyone seeks to answer in life. The first is, who am I? The second is, where is my place in the world? The third is, how do I find it?

"What's most difficult about this is that most people want the answer to the third question before they work on the other two. People who take this shortcut approach seldom find their calling or experience a peaceful career. I have discovered that when the first two questions are answered, 'How do I find it?' is usually easier to do and becomes quite enjoyable. These three questions need to be answered in each new season of life, and the answers do change if we continue to learn and grow."

Cyrus looked at how Darrius had skillfully guided him through the first two questions this day. "I'm beginning to see what you mean," he said as he considered the notes in his journal.

◆◆◆

Hear What Makes You Feel Alive

◆◆◆

What work-related languages do you love to be around?

What words or phrases pique your interests?

Are there any topics that you have always been curious about?

CHAPTER 10

A short time later, as they lay on their bedrolls, Cyrus gazed up at the stars in the clear sky. He thought of his time in the palace with his friends and wondered how they were doing. The hoof beats of camels coming their way interrupted his thoughts.

Cyrus and Darrius stood up, uncertain if they were about to meet up with friends or foes, possibly one of the bands of bandits that roamed the deserts at night. Cyrus kicked dirt and sand toward the fire. The embers still simmered as the two men rushed to hide in a small grove of palm trees a short distance away from the old well.

One of the strangers pulled out a torch and lit it from the embers. As the light grew, Cyrus counted four in a group that had stopped for water and took advantage of this convenient fire. He heard them debating about going on to Jerusalem for the night or staying here. As he listened, he noticed that one of the voices sounded familiar. Then his heart started racing. Gaul. He was here.

Relief swept over Cyrus when he heard them decide to leave and saw them readying to depart. But then Gaul said, "Just a minute. We found a well and a fire. Let me see if there's anything else that would be useful." He began walking toward Cyrus.

As he neared, Cyrus ran out of the grove as fast he could but not fast enough. Aided by the torch and starlight, Gaul saw him clearly. He yelled, "Stargazer! Where you going?" On impulse, Gaul started to run after Cyrus. Then he stopped, shook his ugly head, and laughed in disgust. Gaul turned and got back on his camel, as did his companions. The four rode away.

Darrius never moved from the hiding place in the palms. He remembered what Cyrus had told him about Gaul and made a wise choice to stay out of his way.

Sometime later, Cyrus sneaked back to their camp where Darrius had the fire going again. Cyrus was still shaking, and he was glad to be with his friend. Darrius told him what he'd seen—that Gaul started to run after him but quickly gave up and left.

"What did that mean?" Cyrus wondered. Instead of being thankful for all the good things that happened that day, he went to bed thinking, "Why didn't Gaul try to catch me?" He had a restless night.

The next morning, Darrius and Cyrus both woke very early. As they prepared themselves for the journey ahead, they talked over the events of the night before and what they could mean for Cyrus now. Neither had an answer.

Darrius concluded the matter philosophically. "I have found that trying to figure out why someone does something or does not do something is a waste of time. Instead of assuming the worst and feeling bad, I do something positive. Good feelings follow good action, so let's get moving."

After a short time of brisk walking, Cyrus's mind moved on. He turned to Darrius. "Would you mind if we continue talking about the design of my work mission and a peaceful career? I really need that right now." Before Darrius could answer, people were crowding around them as they entered the wide gate into the city of Jerusalem. They stepped out of the flow of the crowds, and

Darrius said, "Yes, we will discuss that, and there are some people you need to meet today who can help you as well."

Cyrus looked around and saw small groups of men and women sitting around tables on terraces and patios that overlooked the city.

As Darrius explained, people of similar professions gathered at certain tables while others sat around other tables eating breakfast and discussing their day. Bread bakers, jewelers, tailors, seamstresses, café owners, trinket sellers, hat makers, shop merchants, teachers, religious leaders, physicians, innkeepers, fortune-tellers, and spice and herb dealers—all were enjoying the camaraderie of their profession. Friendly debates and laughter filled the air.

Darrius stopped at a group of potters—his profession—and stayed with them until the members of the group went off to their work. He told Cyrus to walk around some more and spend a few minutes with several other groups. Cyrus did. He found the groups very welcoming. He was offered some sweet bread or fresh fruit at most tables. He remembered what Darrius had said about discovering his career interest by recognizing the words or subjects he loved. So, he listened carefully to what the group he was with was talking about. Then he would excuse himself to find another group.

Cyrus managed to meet with six groups that morning before everyone went on their way. He had a good time and felt that he learned a lot by asking mindful questions and really listening—as Darrius had done with him.

In the groups that he most enjoyed, he asked the person who seemed to be a strong leader if he could stop by and see their business sometime. "Yes" was always the answer, and he wrote their names and places in his journal. He thought, *I will have many things to be thankful for today.* He felt encouraged.

When Cyrus rejoined his elder mentor, Darrius asked him what he had noticed about each group. Cyrus said, "It is as if each profession speaks a different language, almost like a code. Some words I heard made me want to hear more, and I found it hard to leave the group. Others I was ready to leave in a very few minutes. I could tell that my ears liked some words but not others."

"Did you take good notes?"

"Yes, I did. I like to draw, so I doodled a picture of each group and wrote notes about the topic each of the groups talked about. I just circled the three groups I enjoyed most." Darrius looked at the page in the journal.

"Title that page 'My Interests,'" Darrius said with a grin.

Darrius and Cyrus walked with a steady pace, arriving in Bethlehem just before noon. As they took a short rest on a bench under a shade tree, Cyrus asked, "Will you help me finish my plan before we reach your home?"

"Most certainly," Darrius responded. As he reviewed what Cyrus had written so far, he said, "You have all the parts. Just put it in an order that makes sense to you and be sure to add one more part, like the last part on my plan."

"What's that?"

"Perhaps you have reasoned by now that your plan is not just to help you get a clearer picture of your best work, but it is also a tool to help other people know how they can help you. You want to write about that as the last part of your plan."

Cyrus wrote the final section, *How You Can Help*. Then he held his plan up to take a look.

"How does that feel?" Darrius asked.

"Peaceful… and scary," Cyrus said. As he looked closely at his plan, he had a sinking feeling that by deciding what he wanted, he may have eliminated some other good possibilities. He would learn more about the power of making a decision over the next few weeks.

"Come," Darrius said. "We have just a little way to go." A short distance away, Darrius opened the front gate and walked up a smooth stone path toward a grand house. "We are home," he said.

Cyrus's Career Search Plan
Blue "Sapphire Stone" Buttons

Background and Current Situation:

Experience working in inns, managing front desk and serving guests

Apprenticed in a government office for a few months

Homeschooled in reading, writing, and numbers

Skills, Interests, and Work Values:

Planning, developing practical ways to improve services and products, training/teaching, ability to see the big picture, offering creative customer service

Work with adults facing complex decisions and working with them one on one or in small groups

Workplace with lots of variety and different people to work with every day; value creative expression, self-determined schedule, and serving a real need

Places that fit me:

Live near Jerusalem and work with a...

1. Top-quality retail or wholesale dealer
2. Community or religious organization
3. Inn or hostel

How you can help me:

Review my plan and my approach

Suggest names of organizations that fit my goals

Recommend other people I should talk to

◆ ◆ ◆

Create a One-Page Plan

◆ ◆ ◆

Have you ever worked for days to get your resume perfect and even customized it to make it fit that perfect job you saw posted — then wondered why you never got a call?

CHAPTER 11

Standing in the front door of Darrius's home was his wife, Bina. She was exquisite. The couple kissed like lovers, not like old people, and Cyrus blushed. As she stepped away from her husband's embrace, Bina turned and greeted Cyrus with a kind smile while Darrius made introductions.

"How was your trip?" she asked. Cyrus told her some of the highlights of his talks with Darrius and his plan, as well as about the visits to the groups in Jerusalem. He realized how excited he was and was afraid he had been a little too enthusiastic and long-winded for first meeting Bina. He stopped talking and asked about her family.

Bina spoke of her children and their families and then followed with questions about his family back home. Cyrus's voice quivered as he spoke of the loved ones he had not seen in a while.

Darrius brought Cyrus's attention back to business. "Now that you have your plan roughed out, you need to go and talk with people about it. You can start with Bina. She loves to give advice."

Darrius laughed as Bina responded, "My husband, the great joker. I see he has helped you with your plan. I'd love to see it tomorrow. Also, you need a place to stay until you find your job. We have a room in the back of our home where you can stay as long as you need."

"Thank you," Cyrus said.

Cyrus retreated to the guest room to make himself comfortable, rest from his travels, and think about all of his experiences. The next morning, after a good night's sleep and a delicious hot breakfast, Cyrus sat down with Bina to look over his plan.

"Very nice. You have answered the first two questions clearly," she said, "but before we start, I need to tell you how to use this plan to get a job offer that fits what you have designed here." Bina laid his plan aside and said, "The first rule in using this plan: never put people on the spot with a request they cannot fulfill. That means, for example, do not ask anyone if they know of a job opening or who might be hiring; only ask them for advice. If you do this, you will be led to a job in the most unexpected ways—as if God steps in front of you and guides your path."

Bina's words of faith reminded Cyrus of Lena, and he thought of his mother and her promised prayers.

Bina went on, "When you visit an owner or manager, they know you are looking for work, so don't mention that. Just focus on learning about their business and asking for their ideas and suggestions on your plan. It feels like pressure when you ask people directly about a job. If you do that, people will likely avoid you when you want to come back and talk with them again. But if you ask for advice, they will welcome you with open arms and will tell others about your smart and sincere approach." Bina sensed Cyrus's uneasiness. "You look concerned or maybe a little confused," she said. "This is new to you. Maybe there is a better way to explain this idea."

She picked up a writing pen and said, "The best way for me to explain this approach is with a picture. Do you mind if I draw something in your journal?" Cyrus handed it to her with a smile.

"Most people do not understand how hiring decisions are made," Bina said as she began to draw. "In most businesses, there is a table where the owners and key workers meet to discuss problems and look for solutions. They also talk about opportunities that they expect to happen in the future. These table meetings happen in the workplace and sometimes in the city patios and restaurants, as you experienced in Jerusalem."

"When a big opportunity or problem is agreed on, someone will say something like, 'Do you know anyone working here or maybe someone outside who can help us with this?'

"If you have handled yourself in a clear and courteous manner when you share your plan with people and then follow up with them every week or so afterwards, when they are at that table, someone you spoke with may remember you. The next thing you know, someone will be seeking you out. You'll get a job before they post a job opening. You'll have no competition and usually get better pay."

This seemed odd to Cyrus, but he respected the wisdom of Darrius and Bina. Though he couldn't muster much conviction, he said, "I'll give it a try this way." Nervous about the process, he asked, "So when I meet someone who might be willing to help me, how do I begin the conversation?"

Bina leaned forward, her motherly eyes filled with kindest and resolve. Then she said, "Cyrus, you'll never be at loss of what to say if you never forget this truth. If you ask directly for what you want, you'll likely get advice or less. But if you ask for advice, you likely get more than you imagined."

It took a few minutes for that amazingly simple truth to sink in and for him to see how it fit his goal of finding a job. Cyrus wrote it in his journal this way, "If I ask about job openings, I'll just get advice. But if I ask for advice, I may get a job offer." He read it to Bina. She smiled with pride.

She continued, "I know you want to work in Jerusalem, and Darrius told me you talked with several businessmen there. When you go back to see them, say, 'I don't expect you to know of any job openings or places that are hiring, I just need your advice on my plan.' Hand them the plan. Give them time to read it, then ask the three questions you wrote in the last part of your plan."

The next day, Cyrus found the names and addresses he had written in his journal and headed back to Jerusalem. He was nervous as he met with the first business owner. At the end of their talk, however, he had several possibilities to explore and two more people to talk to. He spoke to those, and they led him to others.

Within a few days, Cyrus had lots of possibilities and two small job offers—one cleaning tables at a restaurant and another in the camel saddle repair shop. These were not the kind of jobs he really wanted, but he continued talking with people. Though he was following the plan, by the end of the week he still had no job and was getting discouraged. He stopped at a well to get a drink of water and sit for a while, and there he heard a familiar voice. Shadan.

"Hello, my friend," said Shadan. "It is a good thing that I did not let you invest in my jewelry business."

Cyrus was irritated by the comment because he knew that not giving Shadan his white shirt was his idea, not Shadan's. He kept silent as Shadan explained, "There is too much competition here in jewelry, so I have opened a new business."

Cyrus rolled his eyes, unimpressed by the lack of commitment. Then Shadan went on to say, "I help people find good jobs the easy way. No more going from business to business all day begging for work and getting rejected. For just a few coins I will find anyone a terrific job in very little time. I know everyone in town, and they trust me to help them find good people quickly." Cyrus's interest grew. He was intrigued.

"Have you found a job yet?" Shadan asked.

"No," Cyrus said, shaking his head.

"You look very tired. Wouldn't you like to just relax most of the day and let me do the work for you? What do you say, my good friend?"

There was something about Shadan that Cyrus did not like, but it's true that he was tired and discouraged. So, he gave Shadan the few coins he had and shook his hand. Cyrus headed back to Darrius's home to rest from his long week.

On his walk, he saw Shadan's signs advertising a list of great jobs on the walls of several streets. People were lined up looking at the job openings and hoping to see their names listed for an interview. As he mingled in the crowd, he heard stories about several people who had found a job in less than a couple of sunsets. All he had to do was come to town each day and check for his name on a list. He began to get excited.

Maybe Shadan is right this time, he thought.

Two more weeks went by, however, and Shadan had found Cyrus no job worth taking. Shadan had an excuse every time.

"You were their second choice... The job was already filled by someone who worked there... I thought the salary was much more than that... You need to learn to interview better... You are too young... You don't have the right experience."

As Shadan's excuses piled up, Darrius kept asking Cyrus questions about his search. Cyrus was ashamed to tell him and Bina about his decision not to use his plan and take the easy road instead. He gave vague answers as the discouragement set in heavily. That night he wrote two things in his journal: "Never pay anyone to find you a job, unless you want to stay depressed all the time. I am thankful that Darrius and Bina still believe in me."

The next day, something amazing happened.

CHAPTER 12

Early the next morning, Cyrus was walking past a patio on the way to Jerusalem when he saw the owner of the finest hotel, a man he had talked to about his plan. The owner waved him over, offered him a cup of goat's milk, and asked what job he had found.

"Since I had not heard from you, I assumed you were gainfully employed," the hotel owner said. Cyrus cringed in his heart when he recalled he had not followed up as Bina had instructed.

"Not yet," Cyrus admitted. "I have not had much luck in my search."

The hotel owner responded, "This may be your lucky day. I have a small inn in Bethlehem with an opening. My manager there has just been promoted to run my grand hotel here in Jerusalem. With so many visitors coming because of the national census, I will be missing lots of business in Bethlehem if I don't get someone there today. Would you like the job?"

Cyrus was shocked by this unexpected opportunity and didn't know what to say.

The owner continued, "The main reason I am offering this chance to you is because of your gracious and thoughtful approach when you came to visit me. I told several of my business friends about you, and several are looking for you to offer you employment. I think God's favor is shining on both of us today."

The hotel owner had another reason for his interest that he did not share with Cyrus. He knew Alborz and knew of his successful businesses and the type of person he was. He hoped that Cyrus had inherited some of his father's traits and business sense.

"Yes, I will take the job," Cyrus said, "but as I go back to Bethlehem, may I stop to thank my friend and his wife for their hospitality and start late this evening?"

"By all means, yes."

Cyrus hurried as fast as he could back to Darrius and Bina. Huffing and puffing from his dash to their home, he began telling the news almost as soon as Bina greeted him at the front door, but she held up a hand. "Come in, catch your breath, and sit with Darrius and me, so that we both may hear together."

The three settled in the gathering room, and Cyrus told of his good fortune in running into the hotel owner and how others were looking for him too.

"Wonderful news," Bina said.

"Wonderful indeed," Darrius added. "Your preparation has paid off."

Cyrus was hesitant to confess his mistake in trusting Shadan, but he felt it was important to acknowledge error. "I wanted to take the easy way," he explained, "but I found the easy way turns out to be a waste of time and money."

Darrius said, "Many people learn that same truth—sometimes over and over. It is actually a blessing to learn so early that the shortcuts often take longer, and great deals usually cost a great deal more. May you always remember and not have to learn the lesson again."

Bina interrupted. "You have a long night ahead, and we will not send you on an empty stomach. Sit with us and let's enjoy a grand dinner together."

Cyrus ate slowly that night. He was nourished by the meal but even more by the hospitality and care of this kind couple. He really needed to start his journey but didn't want to leave this warm house. His mind wandered to when he and his mother would sometimes wash dishes together and talk after dinner. To buy a little more time there, or maybe it was homesickness, he asked Bina, "May I help you clean up these dishes?"

She was surprised at his request since she knew he was in a hurry. But her motherly instinct came to life. "Why yes, that would be a great help." They stood side by side at the basin.

As he picked up the first plate to wash it, he noticed the BD etched on the bottom. "I have seen this mark before," he said. "It was on some pottery I found in the cave where I met your husband. I think I've also seen it on plates and cups at the palace."

Bina said, "Yes, my dear. Those are products of the business that my husband and I started many years ago, which now belongs to our son and daughter. The mark is a symbol of our work and life together—Bina and Darrius. BD is our business mark."

Then Cyrus realized that his chance meeting of Darrius in the cave might not have been chance at all. The water jug and cooking pot he found buried there must have belonged to Darrius. Cyrus reasoned that Darrius must have stayed in the cave often on his business trips. Most likely Cyrus was not the first young man he had helped find his way.

With the sun setting in the west, he headed east for his new job at the inn. He walked with confidence.

As the days went by, Cyrus threw himself into his work. The work at the inn was hard, and he was spent at the end of each day. Yet he thrived. He recalled those conversations during mealtimes with his father when Alborz had told him things about his work in the inns. Here he was learning even more clearly about the upsides and the downsides of the inn business.

Both good and bad things happened every day. On a really stressful day, it was easy to focus on negatives. But he remembered what his parents and Darrius said to him. "Whatever you focus on expands." He wrote this in his journal.

The inn where he worked was not a series of nice rooms with walls like the Grand Hotel in Jerusalem. It was one large open room where individual sleeping spaces were separated by merely a long cloth hung between them. These open rooms were rife with misfits and misdeeds. Thievery, drunkenness, and profanity were commonplace. Cyrus would never want anyone he cared about to stay in a place like this, but as long as they were strangers with coins in their pockets, what did it matter? That was what was important to the owner, and he needed this job.

As Cyrus grew more comfortable in his role, he found he could lend a listening ear at times. Someone would share a problem or concern. When this happened, he would tell a bit of his story. But then, as Darrius had shown him, he would let the other person tell their story, which often helped that person find a better answer to a problem they were facing. He called this approach "The Darrius Dialogue." He even helped one or two guests think about a plan for finding their own place in the world, and this assistance had come quite naturally to him.

As the owner had predicted, business was brisk, and the inn stayed full. Cyrus found himself enjoying the work. Though he had to occasionally respond to the requests of guests, their demands were minimal, and he was largely able to set his own schedule as the guests did as they pleased.

Many of the things he had written on his plan he was finding in or fashioning into this job. His creative energies were freed, and he could direct them at making improvements. He drew out some plans to improve and expand the business, but it being so busy now, he knew he'd have to wait a while to put them into place.

The next afternoon, something unusual happened.

◆ ◆ ◆

Don't Ask for a Job, Ask for Advice

◆ ◆ ◆

Has anyone ever asked if you could do something for them that you couldn't do? Has anyone ever asked you if you could give them something you had to offer? Which request led you to look forward to talking with them again?

CHAPTER 13

One chilly afternoon Cyrus was busy completing his duties. The room behind him was full of raucous behavior. It seemed like Cyrus had spent the whole day answering the demands of one upset guest after another. As his frustrations grew, he was certain one more interruption might take him over the edge. Then he heard a knock on the door.

"Now what could this be?" he said to himself, annoyed.

When Cyrus opened the door, he was startled to find a decent-looking man escorting a young woman who was obviously great with child. "Pardon me, sir. Do you have room for us to stay the night?" the man asked.

In keeping with the owner's direction, at times like this Cyrus usually would accept the coins required for a night's stay and say, "Come on in, shove somebody out of the way and make room for yourself." But he stopped. For some reason, he didn't want this couple to come inside—not because he didn't like them but because he did. To put this gentle man and his pregnant wife in the room with this rowdy and rough crowd would be risky for them, and in her condition that would be wrong.

"I'm sorry," Cyrus said. "We have no room."

The woman nodded politely, and the man he assumed was her husband seemed to try to hide the concern in his face. But both turned to go. As Cyrus began to close the door, however, he had a moment of inspiration.

"Sir," he called to the man.

"Yes?"

"There's a barn in the back. It may not be the most comfortable place you could stay—and the animals can be a little noisy and smelly—but it does have hay, and you can make a bed for you and your wife. You could rest there and maybe find a better place to stay tomorrow."

"Thank you," the man replied, though Cyrus felt he was surely unhappy about these arrangements for sleeping in a stable given the nearness of childbirth.

"I'm sorry that it's the best I have to offer, but I don't think you'll find anything better tonight."

"I understand," the man said.

Cyrus showed them the spot and helped them settle in. As he returned to the inn, he felt a sense of responsibility to these unusual guests that he could not get out of his mind. Sometime later, he returned to the barn to check on them.

As he walked outside on this cool night, he stepped into an unexpected light. A star overhead shone so brightly it was as if night had become day, and this star seemed to hover over the spot where he had left this couple.

And there he saw the mother, the father, and a baby. Cyrus started trembling at the sight of the baby, overcome by a presence he had never encountered. The birth had clearly taken place only moments before, and the father was helping the mother wrap the baby in strips of cloth, swaddling it as was the custom. He was concerned they did not have enough covering to keep the child warm that cold night.

Cyrus regained his composure. "Wait," he said. "Let me get something else for you." He ran back inside to find a piece of cloth that would be of use. Everything he saw in the inn was soiled. He was at a loss how to help until he remembered. He ran to his quarters and pulled out his old satchel. And there he found his white shirt. He lifted it out of the satchel and dashed back to the couple.

"Here," he said. "You can use this too."

CHAPTER 14

Aaron, Bahram, and Gage hadn't seen Cyrus for more than a year. They had completed their apprenticeships to become astronomers and in some ways, had done well. The king liked them, but Gaul was never on their side. Throughout their apprenticeship, he complained about them every chance he got. Gaul could find the worst in any person, and often they gave Gaul what he was seeking.

Aaron tended to ignore what anyone said and kept pushing task after task. Gage was sticking to the rules, as always, but his over-analysis before a decision of any size was annoying. Bahram irritated people in other ways. He talked too much, bragged too often. Some people said he was too much noise, not much substance.

Even though the men struggled at times, they were astronomers, and there was something different about the night sky that drew their interest. The brightest star they had ever seen had appeared in the east. They discussed it among themselves and with many others, and soon it was the talk of the kingdom.

One day the three of them were called before the king for a special assignment. They were surprised yet also skeptical. Whatever it was, they knew that if Gaul found out, he would surely put a stop to any good opportunity they might receive. The king noticed their hesitancy. He explained that he had many other advisors in the kingdom, and those advisors had told him of their talents and resilience to do their best in a bad situation.

Then the king said, "As we have all seen, there's a brilliant star shining in the distance. What do you think it means?"

Gage spoke with caution. "Sire, we are studying the star and hope to learn what we can."

"What do you know?" the king asked.

Aaron said, "Sire, some have said it is the sign of the birth of a new king."

Bahram added impulsively, "Sire, some believe that someone so honored by the Creator with his own star could hold a new light of truth and wisdom in our world."

The king nodded solemnly. "If this is true, we would like to celebrate this birth." He called over a court official and spoke privately to him before turning again to the three astronomers.

"Now, the three of you will go. If you find this child, anointed by God, ask for his favor on our kingdom and give him a gift. After you deliver this gift, return to the palace, and you each will be elevated in status as royal astronomers, and you will serve me personally."

The court official returned with a package wrapped tightly in a royal cloth and sealed with the king's seal. At the king's direction, the official handed the gift to Gage.

Then the king said, "I am still sad about Cyrus leaving, as I know you are. He was such a gifted boy with wisdom beyond his years. He will always have a place here. I believe he is alive and have heard rumors that he may be near Jerusalem. Look for him along your journey and try to bring him back. I have a special assignment I need him to do for my kingdom."

"Yes, sire," the three men said, bowing. But they remembered Gaul was allowed to hunt down their friend when he disappeared from royal service, and this made them uncertain of the king's real intent.

As the three reverently backed away from the king's throne, Bahram stopped. The king looked at Bahram and nodded, allowing him the opportunity to speak.

Bahram said, "Your Highness, I know it is not proper to question the king, but we are confused. Gaul is your servant. We remember with pain all the things he did, the lies he told us, and the inhumane way he treated people, so we are having a hard time understanding… what is Gaul's role in this plan?"

The king was at first stunned at Bahram's boldness. Then he realized the courage it took to confront a king, and he respected the risk Bahram had taken. The king said, "The word is not out yet, but Gaul is no longer serving me. He left under the veil of night one moon ago, and he now serves another king. A king with no mercy. A king fitted for Gaul."

The king's answer had impact. Aaron, Bahram, and Gage left the chambers certain of the king's confidence and commitment to them. They mounted their camels that day, with the royal gift carefully packed, and left in high hopes of finding the one with his own star. They also hoped to locate their friend and share this good news with him.

A long journey had begun for Aaron, Bahram, and Gage. They trudged over the rugged mountains and then struggled across a vast desert. After a pleasant ride through a lush valley, they forged a small river and arrived in a city. It was Jerusalem, but the star was farther away still. While they were in this large and bustling city, they asked everyone they met about Cyrus. Several people said they had seen him a few months ago, but he was not there now. No one could tell them where he had gone.

Disappointed, they moved on toward where the star had been, and they soon surmised that Bethlehem was the place it shown brightest. When they reached the heart of the small city, they heard rumors that a child had been born to a couple in a barn behind the small inn near the edge of town. They understood that some time had passed since the birth, and by now, the couple had found lodging at a house in town.

"You might try over there," someone suggested, pointing to a simple house that sat on a small side street.

As the men walked toward the doorway, they heard a man's voice say, "It is time." They stepped closer, peeked inside, and saw a woman begin to lean down for her child. The family's belongings were packed as if they were moments away from leaving. As they looked to the child in a handmade crib, they were overcome with an unexplainable awe.

Finally, Aaron spoke. "Excuse us, please." The woman stood up straight, and the couple turned to see the men. There was unmistakable fear in their eyes.

Bahram said, "Don't be frightened. We are here at the request of our king to honor your child and to understand why a star was set in the sky to honor him."

The couple, still frozen in terror, said nothing. Aaron, Bahram, and Gage all took notice of what seemed to be unusually expensive items—a small pouch of gold coins and two other ornate containers—placed in a box near the doorway.

"We are not thieves," said Aaron. "We have a gift for you from our good king."

The couple, sensing their sincerity, relaxed. They all sat down on the hay-covered floor, and the husband told them their story.

"Earlier today," he said, "three astronomers from another king visited us and left the gifts you see in the box. There was a fellow with them, but he stayed outside. He had a hard scowl on his face. He looked in here and then left on his camel as fast as he could go. After he was gone, the magi told us that their king, a jealous and vindictive man, wanted to know where to find our son for one reason only—to destroy him. They told us to move to a safe country as quickly as possible to save our son. We thought that king sent the three of you. Need we say more?"

Aaron, Bahram, and Gage assured the couple they knew of the king but were not from that region. Together they offered their own gift and watched the couple open it.

"A white shirt," the husband and the visitors said at the same time. The husband looked up and noticed the white shirts each of these visitors wore under his robes. He tenderly handed the white shirt to his wife, as the couple and the visitors turned to the child. Aaron, Bahram, and Gage noticed at once the covering that had been placed on the baby like a blanket. They looked to each other with curiosity.

In the silent night, Bahram pointed and whispered to the husband only one word, "Where?"

The husband said, "An innkeeper gave it to us. His inn is a short walk away."

They were reluctant to leave the presence of this child and asked questions about the remarkable star and the child's birth. The father spoke of events few can imagine. At one point, Gage asked the child's name, but the father shook his head, saying, "There will be people looking for him, and we'd rather not say his name."

Though they could have listened forever, the three men knew the family needed to leave for their own safety. Saying their goodbyes, Aaron, Bahram, and Gage stood and headed toward the inn, arriving just after sunset. As they walked inside, they came face-to-face with Cyrus. In delighted surprise, they laughed and hugged. The years apart vanished. The friction they felt at Cyrus's departure was gone. They were friends again.

As the night wore on, the four old friends talked and talked, sharing the joy of reuniting. In great detail, Gage told Cyrus of the king's sadness about his departure and his request for Cyrus to return and serve him in a special role. Cyrus was glad to hear this news.

When their weariness overcame their joy, and they could talk no longer, Cyrus made room for them to stay overnight. The next morning, they sat around a fire together. All were wearing their white shirts, even Cyrus, but his looked different.

Late in the night, the couple had stopped by to return the white shirt he had given them when their baby was born. They told him they had been given another just like it. Because they understood it to be a special shirt, they wanted to return his. Early that morning, he had replaced the white pearl buttons on his shirt with blue sapphire buttons.

"What do the blue buttons mean?" Aaron asked. He knew Cyrus had a plan they all needed to hear.

Cyrus told them his story of the cave, naming all the people he met. He spoke much of Darrius and showed them his career plan. Next, he showed them the color button system he had created. He explained that this system was very significant to help design a peaceful career. But he had to hide some unexpected emotion as he shared with his oldest friends the name of the system. "It's the White Shirt Strategy," he said with a smile and almost a tear.

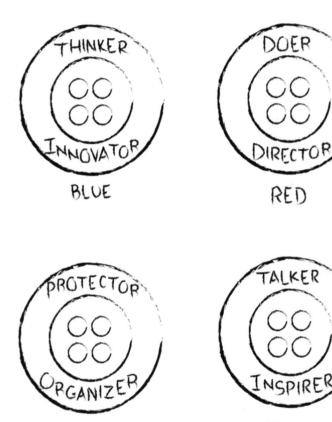

The White Shirt Strategy Button System

Blue Buttons / A Thinker:

- ♦ gets results by planning and innovation
- ♦ likes to strategize, design, facilitate, and plan
- ♦ works best with a lot of reflective time and a self-determined schedule
- ♦ brings more beauty into the world

Red Buttons / A Doer:

- ♦ gets results by directing people to produce
- ♦ likes to build, oversee, and complete projects and get immediate, concrete results
- ♦ works best with challenging work and plenty to do
- ♦ brings more action and products into the world

Yellow Buttons / A Protector:

- ♦ gets results by setting up systems and standards
- ♦ likes to develop standards/guidelines, control quality, analyze, and schedule
- ♦ works best when knows what to do, how work will be carried out and minimal interruptions
- ♦ brings more order into the world

Green Buttons / A Talker:

- ♦ gets results by involving and inspiring people
- ♦ likes to persuade, promote, sell, teach, coach, and negotiate
- ♦ works best with individualized rewards, variety, challenges, clear line of authority, and freedom
- ♦ brings more joy into the world

Cyrus went on to say that after he got the job as innkeeper and had mastered the day-to-day activities that were his primary responsibilities, he had a chance to mingle among and listen to his guests. That's how he learned that some of them did not enjoy the work they were doing. So, he helped them design a plan to find a peaceful, meaningful career.

"The colored buttons became a simple way to identify and acknowledge the type of work the people were designed to do and the places they were most productive," Cyrus said. "For example, carpenters would have red buttons, treasurers yellow, salesman green, and scholars blue."

"What about our buttons?" Aaron asked.

"Can we discover our colors and get a plan?" Bahram asked.

"What do we do?" Gage asked.

Cyrus smiled with great joy and with surprise. At first he was astounded that they were so eager to look inside and question themselves. They were all proud, successful astronomers, and they probably had not been keeping an "Awesome and Awful" journal or thinking much about a new direction. Then he remembered the power of an astonishing experience to inspire a person to change. A truly awe-filled event, such as a magnificent view from a mountain vista, a star over a stable, or a personal encounter like they had in the small house down the street, can create a clearing for seekers to rethink who they are and their place in the world.

Gage, knowing how Cyrus could get lost in his thoughts, said, "Where are you, Cyrus? You didn't answer."

Cyrus recovered quickly. "I would love to help you with that. But it's important to remember that even though I might see what your peaceful career color should be, it's far more important that you discover this for yourselves.

Gage asked, "Should we wait till we get back to the kingdom to do create our plan?"

Cyrus shook his head. "We'll start now. Ready, Set, Go." And he stepped in quick pace with the others in tow.

They retreated to the barn, and Cyrus worked with them that afternoon. Using charcoal from the previous night's fire, the men made notes on the wall of the barn about their family, their interests, their talents, and any other ideas.

There was a lot of information flowing, and they were getting overwhelmed. Thinking is tiring, after all. At sunset, they left the barn, ate a fine dinner, and had a good night's sleep. The ideas on their wall cooked in their minds as they rested.

The next morning, Aaron, Bahram, and Gage looked at the notes with fresh eyes, and it didn't take long for their plans to come together. At lunch they each had a White Shirt Strategy and new colored buttons on their shirts.

Cyrus said, "It's a white shirt because we're all called to do special work and use our talents in our unique way to make the world a better place. No talents are better than others. We have all been endowed with gifts by our Creator to use in this world. You can serve God no matter what you're doing. But it is more fulfilling and more beneficial for others if you are engaged in the work that satisfies your interests and uses your best talents that were born in you."

They each studied their White Shirt Strategy and then shared them with each other.

Gage asked, "Why don't we just list jobs titles on our one-page plans? It seems like that would be proper and clearer for everyone to see what we wanted."

Cyrus replied, "I thought the same thing myself, so I asked Bina, Darrius's wife, who showed me the one-page plan idea. She told me that the purpose of the strategy was to engage people in interesting conversations and get their advice. Specific job titles can restrict people's thinking to only about job openings. You are looking for problems or opportunities that you can help with using talents and abilities, no matter the job title."

Gage was still concerned, though that is how Gage was most of the time—details, details. But the others seemed to understand, and they would all see how well this approach worked soon enough.

Aaron's White Shirt Strategy
(Red "Ruby Stone" Buttons)

Background and Current Situation:

Assisted with office duties in my father's construction and engineering company

Completed all phases of astronomy training and began training others

Experienced in highly visible position, pushing faster completion of projects or products

Skills, Interests, and Work Values:

Building, organizing, overseeing projects to get immediate and concrete results that save time and make money

Capitalize on my practical, decisive, commanding personality to solve complex problems when time is of the essence

In a place where there is plenty to do; freedom to act, implement, and control work; many challenging assignments to enjoy

Places that fit my goals:

Live within fifty miles of the palace and travel often in an organization focused on...

1. Construction
2. Protecting valuable property
3. Engineering

Ways you can help:

Review my plan and advise me on my approach

Suggest names of organizations that fit my fields

Recommend other people I should talk to

Bahram's White Shirt Strategy (Green "Emerald Stone" Buttons)

Background and Current Situation:

Experienced in sales of fine clothes and robes

Completed astronomy training for king

Seeking more challenging work in service of the king

Skills, Interests, and Work Values:

Persuading, promoting, selling, negotiating, mediating, motivating groups to act and people to buy

Apply my enthusiastic, inspirational leadership style and competitive, flexible, and independent approach to move people forward toward a common goal

Work with people who are affluent, business-minded, and/or have political influence

In a workplace that rewards autonomy, individual goals, and accomplishment and has a wide variety of challenges

Places that fit my goals:

Live in large growing city and work in a...

1. Tailor shop and clothing wholesaler
2. Business-to-business service company
3. Government headquarters

How you can help:

Review my plan and my approach

Suggest names of organizations that fit my goals

Recommend other people I should talk to

Gage's White Shirt Strategy
(Yellow "Amber Stone" Buttons)

Background and Current Situation:

Assisted with office duties in my father's bookkeeping business

Completed phases one and two astronomy training for king

Seeking more analytical work to capitalize on my attention to detail

Skills, Interests, and Work Values:

Use my skills in developing standards, setting up systems and quality-control procedures. Working with numbers and details to create an effective administrative system

Fix systems or processes that are broken or coordinate major upgrades to improve overall efficiency

Most productive when there is clarity on what is required, how work will be carried out and evaluated; when I can work in a small group with minimal interruptions

Places that fit my goals:

Live and work within fifteen miles of my hometown with a...

1. Bookkeeping business or accounting office
2. Craftsman who needs someone to determine real cost and set prices to become more profitable
3. Government headquarters

How you can help:

Review my plan and advise me on my approach

Suggest names of organizations that fit my goals

Recommend other people I should talk to

◆ ◆ ◆

Feelings Follow Actions

◆ ◆ ◆

Have you noticed that when you wait for that feeling to come that will motivate you to do something, you seldom act? You stay put or you hit the snooze button again?

But if you take an action or make a move, you automatically feel better—and are sometimes motivated to do even more?

CHAPTER 15

The next morning, Cyrus traveled to the hotel owner's office to express appreciation for the opportunity to work at the inn in Bethlehem and to let him know that he would be leaving the region to return to his homeland. "Is there someone who can take over my position?" Cyrus asked.

"You have done an excellent job for me, Cyrus, and I thank you for your service," the hotel owner said. "Yours will be big shoes to fill, but I will move an apprentice at another inn to that location. He reminds me a little of you, and I know he is ready. In fact, he said that he met you once in Bethlehem and that you helped him with his career plan. This will be a good opportunity for him. Go, my son, and blessings to you in your return home."

Cyrus wrapped up his role as innkeeper, and soon the four friends made their long journey back to their kingdom home. As they approached the palace, the high-tower guards saw them from afar and sent word to the king. The king was waiting at the palace gate with open arms.

"Take some time to rest," he said to Aaron, Bahram, and Gage. "When you're ready to tell your story, I invite you to the chambers to let me hear it." Then he turned to Cyrus. "After I meet with your friends, I will talk with you alone."

Aaron, Bahram, and Gage went to the palace later that day. The temperatures were low, and the wind was cold, so the three men kept their heavy coats on while they sat at the king's dining table. They told about the long trip from the start, often tripping over each other's stories, but finally got to the visit in Bethlehem. Gage shared the details of how the star led them to a baby "king" as predicted. He told of the couple's distress and also of giving the white shirt gift.

The king naturally asked, "What was the baby's name?"

Aaron answered, "The father feared telling us the baby's name because of their need to escape their bad king and hide in another land."

Then Bahram stood to speak. He was nervous, which was unusual for him, the great orator. Yet the others had asked him to explain, as best he could, what the couple said about why their baby had a star. "The couple told us that the night their son was born, some shepherds came to see them. These shepherds said that an angel had spoken and told them that this child had been born to be a savior who would bring the light of truth to the world. The couple said an angel had visited both of them as well with the same message several months before."

The king nodded solemnly as Bahram continued, "There was no pride or sense of privilege as they spoke of being so chosen by God. Theirs was more of assured humbleness. We were all taken aback by this incredible story. We still question it all, but we agreed there was astounding peacefulness when we were in the presence of the child."

The king responded that he was pleased with what they had done and had to say. But everyone could see that he was deep in thought.

The room had warmed considerably since their meeting had begun, and Aaron asked if they could lay their heavy coats aside. As they removed the coats and handed them to the servants, the three astronomers were wearing their white shirts as they usually did—with one big change.

The puzzled king asked, "Why are your shirt buttons colored instead of white as they were designed?"

One at a time, the men told the king about Cyrus's system, and each of them showed him their plans and their gratitude journals. The king said very little, and they were concerned—not knowing if he was angry or was in deep reflection.

As they were excused and left the palace, they saw Cyrus on the street. He asked, "How did your report go?"

"It went well," Aaron said.

"We told the king about your system for helping people find their place in the world of work and the reason for the colored buttons," Bahram offered.

"How did he take it?" Cyrus asked, nervous.

Gage shrugged. "We're not sure."

Aaron said, "Good luck to you. The king wants to meet you tomorrow." He patted Cyrus on the back, but Cyrus remained anxious and didn't rest well that night.

At the appointed time, Cyrus arrived at the palace and was escorted through the hallways toward the king's chambers. He was nearing the doorway as his friend Hester came bounding out.

"Cyrus!" she said with astonishment. "I did not know if I would ever see you again. How are you?"

"I am well, and you?"

"Very well indeed."

"I can see that you are," Cyrus acknowledged. "You look so…" He almost said "beautiful," but he sensed a deeper quality. "You look so joyful."

"Oh, I am, Cyrus. I am overjoyed, in fact. I have had very good news this morning. The king has named me to be the chief astronomer. I am so thrilled. I love the study of the stars."

"That's wonderful, Hester," Cyrus said as he reached to offer a congratulatory hug.

"Thank you, my friend. I'm so excited about telling my parents, I have to rush off. But I hope I'll see you again soon."

"I'll count on it."

As Hester walked quickly away, Cyrus moved from the hallway into the private chambers. The king greeted him warmly but also spoke candidly. He told Cyrus how disappointed he was that he had left. "Your father, Alborz, paid a large sum of money, as had all the white shirt families, to even be considered to receive this honor to serve the king in a royal position," the king said.

"Yes, sire," Cyrus humbly acknowledged.

Even though the king had learned of Gaul's mistreatment, he asked for Cyrus's own explanation for why he left and why he had returned.

Cyrus thought for a moment then said, "Gaul was a factor for my leaving, but the deeper reason was I just did not fit the work I was asked to do. I was not made for this work. I knew that I would never be able to do my best as a servant to you and the kingdom. The reason I returned is because you asked, and I would like to find a new place of service here, if you would have me."

Then the king said, "I am so happy you have returned. Go for now, but come back tomorrow when the sun is at its peak. I will make an announcement to all in my kingdom about you and your friends' new places of service in the kingdom."

CHAPTER 16

Aaron, Bahram, Gage, and Cyrus talked a lot that night and got very little sleep. But each got up early and had breakfast with their parents at their houses. Every family was thrilled to hear of their son's life-changing experiences and grateful for their return home, yet they were anxious about the coming announcement by the king.

As the sun rose to its highest point of the day, the king arrived for the palace assembly. Acclaim of bright horns and cymbals of court musicians announced him. He stepped to the stage and said, "Today is a special day in our kingdom. Our astronomers Aaron, Bahram, and Gage have returned safely from their journey to the star that shone in the east. As I had requested, our astronomers found the baby and gave the parents of 'the One who was honored with his own star' a special white shirt with perfect pearl white buttons—the finest my tailors have ever made. They were asked to present it to this child at his coming of age and to request his blessing on our kingdom."

The crowd was still. The king continued, "There is now on the earth a baby with his own star. The One who placed all the stars in the sky gave that star as a sign of this child's birth. I honored this baby with the astronomers' perfect white shirt, so white shirts with white buttons will never again be given to anyone to recognize them as an astronomer. All who now wear this white shirt must remove it by the end of this day."

Not a sound was heard in the crowd. The astronomers were dumbfounded. Then the king asked Aaron, Bahram, Gage, and Cyrus to step up on the podium stage with him and turn and face the crowd.

The people in front noticed it first. The buttons. Aaron's shirt buttons were red, Braham's green, Gage's yellow, and Cyrus's blue. Murmurs filled the arena. The king went on, "Cyrus, please explain the buttons to my people—and how they came to be."

Cyrus cleared his throat, unsure of what he was about to say. Then the words started to flow. He described his journey and how he went away seeking to find his best place of service, and what he had learned he could now share with others. He explained the color system and how the whole process was designed to help people find their true colors and find their best place of service.

When Cyrus had completed his explanation, the king took the stage again. "Like all kings," he said, "I want to have a great kingdom, but my goal is not to lead by fear. I have seen how other kings act. They try to control people and pressure them to serve their own selfish desire to build their empires to rule the world.

"History shows that their reigns have all fallen, and their people crushed. I have been searching for a way to help each of my people live in true freedom—to be given the opportunity to learn to use your gifts and talents, find work that matters to you and others, have a better life and happier and healthier families. When this happens, ours will be a strong kingdom."

The king continued, "Cyrus had the courage to run from what others wanted him to do and in doing so found himself and his mission and career calling. I declare that Cyrus is now the official overseer of the White Shirt Strategy for my kingdom.

"From this day forward, all who want it will be helped to design a peaceful, purposeful career, and every person in the kingdom—boy, girl, man, or woman—at their request and with their effort can receive a white shirt. And this shirt will come with buttons that symbolize their best place of service along with a small journal to remind them of the secret to true career peace—being thankful each day.

"Aaron, Bahram, and Gage will serve the king in their career colors on the buttons of their shirts. Aaron (ruby red) will be in charge of palace engineering and oversee all construction. Bahram (emerald green) will be the king's official spokesman and new chancellor. Gage (gold) will keep careful watch over the royal treasury."

That night Cyrus, Aaron, Bahram, and Gage sat in front of a campfire, overjoyed about their jobs and plans. They were now adults but felt like young boys again. After a while, Aaron, Bahram, and Gage went to their homes. But Cyrus stayed. He sat by the glowing coals, leaned back, looked up at the stars, and wondered, how would he begin and manage his big new role as leader of the White Shirt Strategy?

CHAPTER 17

Cyrus's self-doubt soon shifted to confidence as he quickly found amazing success in his new role. People were benefiting beyond their expectations. White shirts with colored buttons were seen everywhere. White Shirt Strategies were being discussed on the patios and business tables around the city.

However, it didn't take long for him to realize that he needed help. He knew he was very able to help younger people discover their color and move into a good job fit. But middle-aged and older people needed help too. He was not yet prepared for someone who needed guidance to move up in their career, or retire with a good repurpose plan, or, most difficult of all, someone who had not worked in a while and wanted to relaunch their career.

Fortunately, he knew just the man to ask for help.

Darrius traveled this area several times a year to help with his family's business. On those trips, he lodged in the palace and provided guidance for people who were retiring from successful careers and needed to repurpose or relaunch.

But even with the fast advancements and with Darrius's help, the work proved to be larger than they could tackle together. Cyrus hired some apprentices, and that was when he recognized that he needed a process. With a simple process in place, others could follow it as they helped their clients design their career strategies. Everyone could stay on track and help each other find their way better and faster.

The White Shirt Strategy process that Cyrus designed is based on three questions. The questions need to be answered in order, and there is personal work to be done to help discover your best answers for each one. This is the process:

First question: Who am I?

Personal work: Record what you are thankful or not thankful for each day for seven days and jot down all your career ideas and big dreams. Draw your family career tree and/or list the work you have done in your past. Ask people who know you to share their ideas on your strengths. Keep notes of your ideas and insights.

Second question: What is my place?

Personal work: List your top career interests, natural strengths, and values. Explore career fields that fit all or most of your interests, strengths, and values. Make a short list of those places.

Third question: How do I find it?

Personal work: Create a one-page written plan from the work you did with questions one and two. Visit people you know well, show them your plan, and ask for advice and referral to others who might help. This will lead you to your ideal work.

Cyrus created a working journal for people to use, based on the three questions and work assignments. The White Shirt Strategy working journal can be used for any career transition situation or season of life a person happens to be in. The questions are the same, but some of the assignments may be different according to a person's age and experience.

This journal and process worked well, but as was his nature, Cyrus wanted to find the most effective and efficient approach. He experimented with having people work in small groups of ten, then he tried five in a group and finally three, but there were always scheduling issues and some people would get ahead or behind. It was messy and difficult, but he didn't give up. He knew there had to be a better approach.

In his tests and trails he noticed a couple of patterns:

First, people tend to form in twos, even in a group setting. No matter the size of the group, people would naturally find one person with whom they worked best and partner with her or him. He observed that this partnership worked even better if the pair had some guidelines to help them work together, rather than if they were left to create their own approach.

Second, differences can produce a better outcome. Cyrus noticed that oftentimes when someone worked with a person with different colored buttons, they got more done and the outcome was better for both. It wasn't always true, but since Red and Yellow tend to focus more on tasks and Green and Yellow are drawn to focus more on people, it made sense that their differences would complement. He decided that this was not a strategy he would insist on, but it was something he would certainly encourage when the situation evolved naturally.

Based on all his research, Cyrus designed the White Shirt Strategy process to capitalize on partners working together with instructions on how to have an effective conversation—a dialogue guide. Using this one-on-one approach and structured method, both partners usually completed their plans in a week or two. (If pairs took more than two weeks, they lost momentum and seldom completed their plans.) Plus, Cyrus found that the two people naturally wanted to stay in touch after their plans were completed. Some even made a pact to support each other during the ups and downs of their search. He was always excited to hear about happy celebrations that partners often held when they landed in their place in the world.

This is how the White Shirt Strategy process came to work back then. It still works this way today.

> Are you fresh out of college or near graduation and need a plan to land a good job?
>
> Have you hit a plateau in your career and want to make big shift in the way you work?
>
> Are you at retirement age but still have more to give and want to repurpose your work life?
>
> Have you intentionally taken a period of time off work and decided now it's time to get a job?
>
> Have you lost your job and need to find another sooner than later?

Would you like to design your White Shirt Strategy and make your next career move your best move? Part II shows you how to do this in seven clear steps. But don't try this alone. Find a friend, peer, colleague, mentor, pastor, parent, grandparent, or career coach who will read this book and work with you through the working journal that follows and the workbook available at whiteshirtbook.com.

Which button color would be on your white shirt?

Visit whiteshirtbook.com now and take the My Button Color Quiz to find out.

PART II

*The White Shirt
Strategy Guide*

THE WHITE SHIRT STRATEGY GUIDE
A Step-by-Step Guide to Build Your One-Page Personal Career Strategy in One Week with a Dialogue Partner

You may be wondering why Cyrus's ancient approach to finding an ideal career works so well today. The answer—we have come full circle.

Consider this. Two thousand years ago, there were very few job titles. Well, there was "king," but those opportunities were limited to one per country. There were servants to the king with the job title of "astronomer," but you'll clearly notice that that position was not a good fit for many people.

Instead, when Cyrus began to seek career satisfaction, he looked for a field that could use his skills and fit his interests. He was a "knowledge worker" or "freelancer" moving from place to place plying his talents. As he sought his next move, Cyrus focused on talking about his skills and letting his advisors create the title or job name that fit what he did.

Job searches looked this way for over one thousand years.

In the 1800s to early 1900s, the agricultural age, most people were farmers or project workers who built things—houses, barns, buildings, and tools. As the industrial age evolved so did job titles—factory jobs, management jobs, administrative workers, medical positions, etc. Some of this "job title focus" is still here as we move into the knowledge-based, high-tech economy, and most career advisors still promote looking for a particular position.

However, the way we work within organizations is changing again, and studies predict that, by 2030, one third of workers will be freelance workers. They will be selling their skills to organizations who are creating jobs on the fly. Most jobs will be project-based, knowledge work that will be generated from opportunities and challenges facing rapidly changing organizations.

Given that the end of jobs as we have known them (and named them) is near—some would say it is already here—this is the perfect time to apply this time-tested approach to finding your place in the world of work today.

A Time-Tested System

The White Shirt is set a long time ago, but it's far less about history than it is about your own future. In this imaginative illustration, for example, you didn't have to be wealthy to have a journal in which to record your thoughts (in a day when paper and ink were rare and expensive). Yet recording your thoughts is important if you want to design your own career. The principles used by Cyrus and his buddies will help you, and the seven-step working journal that follows will give you space to make notes and jot down ideas.

Cyrus devised an excellent system, but I'm sure he won't mind that it has been updated for a modern audience. In particular, the White Shirt website at whiteshirtbook.com will help you along your journey. Please visit this website as you undertake this process. There is a downloadable workbook with exercises that accompany each step of the journey, as well as other helpful resources. You will also find real examples of career plans created by several of my clients who were in different stages of life and work.

There's also a link on the website to provide feedback, and I hope you'll let me hear from you and let me know your progress. Feel free to ask questions or offer suggestions that would make it easier for the next person.

Remember, it is better not to take this journey alone. Get a dialogue partner to agree to work and think with you as you seek to answer the three questions: Who am I? Where is my place in the world? How do I find it?

Who could this other partner be? I can envision a grandparent entering retirement working through the White Shirt Strategy with a grandchild just completing college. Or a recent graduate working with someone experiencing midcareer dissatisfaction. Or a husband and wife who need a way to talk about the next phase in their life and work. The partnership may be a mentor and mentee, or two people in the same circumstances working together. Regardless, choose someone you trust as a dialogue partner to join you, with each of you reading *The White Shirt* and working through your own journal together.

To choose your partner, think creatively about people from your graduating class, in your family, from your church, in your professional circles, or in your social circle. It could be a friend you think is in the same boat, or someone further along who is tired of steering the same old ship.

Even if you are a part of a group study of *The White Shirt*, having a partner in the group or outside will be the key to your success.

As it says in the Bible, "Two are better than one because they have a good return for their labor. For if either of them falls, the one will lift up his companion. But woe to the one who falls when there is not another to lift him up" (Ecclesiastes 4:9–10 NASB).

There are three different options that you and your partner can choose from to apply the principles in this story to your career:

1. Read a few chapters at a time and discuss the questions that are listed on the pages where the nine principles are highlighted. Then you might want to do some of the exercises in the workbook at whiteshirtbook.com to help you develop your one-page plan.

2. Get a group of six to eight people together and find a leader who will commit to meet four times to work through the book. A four-week small group leader's guide is available to download at The White Shirt book website.

3. Or follow the one-week or seven-step process detailed here:

What the One Week Journey Looks Like

1. Read *The White Shirt* and visit the book website.

2. Have a friend read *The White Shirt*.

3. Review *The White Shirt Strategy Guide* together.

4. Agree that you would like to work alongside each other for the defined length of time to develop your plan. The seven steps on following pages can be done in the next seven days or fourteen days or somewhere in between. If you take more time fourteen days to complete, people lose momentum and don't finish.

So, agree on a time frame together. Note: if you work in a small group, this will be a four-week process.

5. Remember that you will be working as a dialogue partner, not a coach or mentor. You will have equal roles as you walk along together—being a listening ear, sounding board, and a support for each other.

6. Choose to keep this process private. It's almost as if you are going into your cave. *The White Shirt* story illustrates this concept.

Daily activities are suggested for each step. There are also specific assignment suggestions for particular steps. The daily activities listed in the journal pages include the following:

Record a few things you are most thankful for or were awesome each day for the first five steps. These will be events, actions, or activities you were involved in that gave you energy.

Record a few things you were least thankful for or were awful each day for the first five steps. These will be events, actions, or activities you were involved in that pulled energy from you.

Write or draw your ideas, dreams, and random thoughts about your next move as you complete each step.

As another helpful activity, spend time in nature—without your headset on. Look and listen for awesomeness as you walk a forest trail, stroll a beach or lake front, climb a hill or mountain, view a sunrise or sunset, or sit under a night sky full of stars.

The one-week journey will break down as follows:

First Section Guides You to Answer: *"Who am I?"*

Know What You Don't Want: You will have noticed that I included several statements within Cyrus's story that are the principles underlying the White Shirt Strategy. The first is "Know What You Don't Want." For some of you, you will have already gotten to this point through your career experiences. Others of you are only beginning to sense your concern about taking the wrong path. Knowing what you don't want creates an awareness that can lead you to productive action. As you prepare for your journey, give thought to what you don't want, and that leads into the next principle.

Take A Bold Step: Before you begin, complete your statement of "why this is a good time." Contact your dialogue partner to talk about how you will help each other stay on track during your timeframe commitment. Review the Darrius Dialogue Guide.

Acknowledge Your Original Design: Complete your self-perception worksheet then invite a few people who know you well to write you a note or tell you about your gifts and talents.

Parents, Peers, and the Past Matter: Compile your family tree exercise. Then fill in your work history matrix and/or hobby/learning chart.

See Your Invisible Skills: Write about a few projects or achievements you are proud of. Examine them to spot your transferable skills and career values.

Review what you learned over the last three steps. Then complete the top portion or left side of your one-page Career Strategy draft. Contact your dialogue partner and review the work you completed.

Second Section Guides You to Answer: *"Where is my place in the world? And how do I find it?"*

Hear What Makes You Feel Alive: Choose between several career interest worksheets that will help you identify industries or business fields that fit who you are.

Create a One-Page Plan: Complete the bottom portion or right side of your White Shirt Strategy. Look at your plan as a whole, in light of all the work you have completed in your exercises and in your journal pages. Adjust as needed.

Don't Ask for a Job, Ask for Advice: Make a list of the five people you may want to share your plan with. Send thank you notes to everyone who wrote about their perceptions of your gifts and talents. Read the "How Do I Find it?" information on the website.

Feelings Follow Actions: After you finish your plan, meet with your dialogue partner to discuss it. Talk about how you will support each other in the "How do I find my ideal work?" stage.

Connect with your Dialogue Partner at least once a week and discuss your progress in your action plan and share notes from your journal pages.

Please visit whiteshirtbook.com and look at some recent White Shirt Strategy plans. Be sure to download the workbook so that you will have the exercises handy as you begin creating your plan on the pages that follow. For those of you who would rather not write in your book, simply download the workbook and use those pages instead. The White Shirt Strategy Workbook contains all the pages that follow and the exercises, as well as links to the videos—everything you will need to complete your personal White Shirt Strategy is at whiteshirtbook.com.

Getting Started

Now, as you and your partner prepare to begin your journey, take a moment to learn about the Darrius Dialogue that follows. From there, you will have pages for each step of your journey to record your notes. Remember, a workbook and other resources will be found at whiteshirtbook.com. It may be helpful if you get a folder or notebook to keep your worksheets in one place or a wall where you can put sticky notes of all your ideas—like the wall in Cyrus's cave.

The Darrius Dialogue Guide

The Darrius Dialogue Guide was given this name because Darrius, in *The White Shirt*, had an uncommonly effective manner of interacting with others. He did this in such a way that allowed each person to find his or her answers, own those answers, and feel more confident to act. This model can help you and your dialogue partner act as Darrius for each other. Please discuss this with your partner at the onset of your one-week journey together.

See the Dialogue Guidelines for talking and listening on the following page.

Dialogue Guidelines:

If you are talking:	
Do:	**Do Not:**
Say what you think, feel, or have done without trying to defend it.	*Do not* dwell on the past.
	Do not ask for advice from your dialogue partner now.
Talk about yourself without worrying what the other person may think about you.	*Do not* look for approval (or lack of approval) from your dialogue partner.

If you are listening:	
Do:	**Do Not:**
Pay very careful attention to what your dialogue partner is saying.	*Do not* interrupt.
If you don't understand something that she/he has said, simply ask, "Can you say a little more about?"	*Do not* give advice or appear to be an expert. In particular, refrain from saying, "Here's what I think you should do," or anything else that implies that you have *the* answer.
Take notes. Read notes out loud, and then hand or send your notes to him or her.	

When you end your dialogue as listener, you may want to ask something like this:

What do you plan to do with what we talked about here?

Can I do anything to support you?

Before You Begin
Know What You Don't Want
Take a Bold Step

"Why is now a good time for me?"   Date: _____

Today I will:

❏ Write my "why this is a good time" statement. Examples of how to write these statements are on the next page and at whiteshirtbook.com.

❏ Talk with my dialogue partner. Review my plans for the week and set a date for our retreat at the end of this process. Discuss the Darrius Dialogue Guide.

❏ View the "Before You Begin" video at whiteshirtbook.com.

Awesome – I am most thankful for (gave me energy):

Awful – I am least thankful for (drained my energy):

Bright Ideas, Random Thoughts, and Doodles

Why is now a good time for me?

Write a few sentences here that explains where you are and why this is a good time for you to make a plan for a career move:

Fill-in-the-Blank Examples:

After completing my college degree or training (and working internships at _____), I'm also really interested in the looking at _____ field or area.

After five years working in _____, I am getting bored and need a new challenge but would really like to stay with my current company and move to a new area.

After working ten years as a _____, my company is cutting back on staffing, and I fear I will be let go. I think the safest thing to do is to look for a job with another company, but I also have a desire to work for myself.

After _____ years as a _____, I hit a wall last _____ and decided to change careers.

After twelve successful years in _____, I find myself unfulfilled and want to find a more satisfying career, as well as a sense of purpose and clarity on what I wanted to do.

After working for twenty years in the _____
industry, I have decided to explore starting my own company.

After thirty years in the _____ field, I'm ready to
retire, but I'm not ready to sit still. I need something to do that
will be meaningful and keep me active.

STEP 1 — Who am I?   Date:_____

Acknowledge Your Original Design

Today I will:

- ❏ Complete my self-perception worksheet. This "As a Child" exercise is on the next page and in the workbook at whiteshirtbook.com.

- ❏ Ask three people who know me well to complete the "My Perception of You" form. This form is also available on the website. In addition, when these forms are returned, you will want to complete the worksheet where you record what you learned from yourself and others.

- ❏ View the Step 1 video at whiteshirtbook.com.

Awesome – I am most thankful for (gave me energy):

Awful – I am least thankful for (drained my energy):

Bright Ideas, Random Thoughts, and Doodles

My Ideal Work Environment – As a Child

Instructions: Please circle *one or two of the four choices* in each section (A, B, and C) below that best describe you as a young child. Feel free to add words and eliminate words or terms to make this fit you. Do this as if you were looking back and observing yourself before or during your elementary school years.

A. Interests: a person's innate aptitude and natural inclination

When this child is immersed in play, I see her/him drawn to:

1. Building something tangible

2. Persuading others to join in

3. Analyzing and organizing objects or numbers

4. Inventing a new or better way

He/she also appears to want to bring or create more:

1. Beauty: by being artistic, innovative, and creative

2. Happiness: by generating laughter and excitement

3. Order: by making things work better or more effectively

4. Action: by getting lots of things done quickly and leading

B. Personality Strengths: positive traits that show up consistently when we are at our best

When this child is at her/his best, I would describe her/him as:

1. Practical, decisive, direct
2. Enthusiastic, competitive, flexible
3. Loyal, cooperative, cautious
4. Perceptive, reflective, insightful

C. Motivating Environment: the elements that support or aid us in being our best

This child is most motivated when he/she has:

1. Autonomy in setting and achieving goals and lots of variety
2. Plenty to do and challenging problems to solve
3. Reflective time alone and freedom from constant social interaction demand
4. Straight forward instruction and minimal interruptions and change

Which of the elements you circled are still true today?

Send out "My Perception of You" Worksheets

The "My Perception of You" Worksheet for others to complete should be distributed to three or four people who know you well today. Before you email the worksheet to them, I suggest that you phone them. Ask if they will do this today or tonight and send it back to you by the next day at noon. Go to whiteshirtbook.com to download this sheet.

STEP 2 — **Who am I?**   **Date:** _____

Parents, Peers, and Past Matter

Today I will:

- ❏ Complete my family career tree as tall (far back) and as wide (extended family and close family friends) as possible. (Samples are available in your workbook.)

- ❏ Fill in my history of work, hobbies and/or things I love to learn about (Student, mid-career and retirement samples are in the workbook).

- ❏ View the Step 2 video.

Awesome – I am most thankful for (gave me energy):

Awful – I am least thankful for (drained my energy):

Bright Ideas, Random Thoughts, and Doodles

STEP 3 — Who am I?   **Date:**_____

See Your Invisible Skills

Today I will:

- ❏ Look back over the work history, hobbies, and/ or things I loved to learn about chart that I completed in Step 2.

- ❏ Think about three or four projects I accomplished/ achieved and enjoyed and am proud of. Write a short sentence or two about each accomplishment. (See samples in the workbook.)

- ❏ Complete the Career Values exercise found in the workbook.

- ❏ View the Step 3 video.

Awesome – I am most thankful for (gave me energy):

Awful – I am least thankful for (drained my energy):

Bright Ideas, Random Thoughts, and Doodles

STEP 4 — Who am I?   Date:_____

Today I will:

- ❏ Review and summarize what I learned from my thankfulness exercise over the past five steps.

- ❏ Complete the top portion or left side of my White Shirt Career Strategy Draft 1. (Find the worksheet in the workbook.)

- ❏ Contact my dialogue partner and check in.

- ❏ Send a thank you note, text, or email to the people who completed the "My Perception of You" form.

- ❏ Read over the material I will be working on for Step 5.

- ❏ View the Step 4 video.

Awesome Summary – Looking back over the last five steps, the four or five most recurring things I was thankful for (gave me energy) were:

Awful Summary – The four to five most common things I was least thankful for (drained my energy) were:

This is what I learned about what I need to be self-motivated when I am working:

STEP 5 — Where is my place in the world? Date: _____

Hear What Makes You Feel Alive

Today I will:

- ❏ Review the worksheets in the workbook for Step 5 and work on the ones that seem right for me.

- ❏ Complete the worksheet(s) I chose and make notes on industries that fit my interests.

- ❏ View the Step 5 video.

Awesome – I am most thankful for (gave me energy):

Awful – I am least thankful for (drained my energy):

Bright Ideas, Random Thoughts, and Doodles

STEP 6 — **Where is my place in the world?** **Date:**_____

Create a One-Page Plan

Today I will:

- ❏ Identify two to three industries that fit the topics or subjects I am most interested in and want to pursue. (A list of industries and tools on how to identify industry fields is available in the workbook.)

- ❏ Identify my geographic preference (where I'd like to live and work).

- ❏ Choose three to five organizations that fit my industry and geography and list them on my plan.

- ❏ Complete the bottom portion or right side of my one-page plan.

- ❏ View the Step 6 video.

Awesome – I am most thankful for (gave me energy):

Awful – I am least thankful for (drained my energy):

Bright Ideas, Random Thoughts, and Doodles

STEP 7 — How do I find it?   Date:_____

Don't Ask for a Job, Ask for Advice

Today I will:

- ❏ Make a list of the five people with whom I plan to share my plan.
- ❏ Read the "How do I find it?" information in my workbook.
- ❏ Reread chapters 11 and 12 in *The White Shirt*.
- ❏ View the Step 7 video.

Awesome – I am most thankful for (gave me energy):

Awful – I am least thankful for (drained my energy):

Bright Ideas, Random Thoughts, and Doodles

STEP 8   Date:_____

Feelings Follow Actions
After you complete your plan

Today I will:

❏ Meet with my dialogue partner to share and discuss my and his/her work and help each other design our individual strategies.

❏ Review the Darrius Dialogue Guide.

❏ Tell each other the names of the first three people we will show our plan to, and talk about what to do and not do in our White Shirt Strategy meetings.

❏ Discuss how we will support each other in our "How do I find it?" phase.

❏ Follow "The 5 Second Rule" to stay motivated and find the career I want. (See more on the next page.)

❏ View the Step 8 video.

Awesome – I am most thankful for (gave me energy):

Awful – I am least thankful for (drained my energy):

Bright Ideas, Random Thoughts, and Doodles

THE 5 SECOND RULE
How to Stay Motivated and Find the
Career You Want

By the time you are reading this, you should have your plan in hand and be ready to begin sharing it and researching through your network. But there's another hurdle to overcome.

Job search is difficult. It is change. It is personal. It feels scary to everyone. Sure, it feels better right now to stay in bed, hit the snooze button ten times, sit at your desk for hours filling out job applications, or tweak your resume for the fiftieth time instead of picking up the phone and calling a friend and asking for advice. Maybe you'll feel like taking these steps tomorrow.

You won't. You don't "feel" your way into acting. You act first and the feeling to act follows, and it grows. Momentum is a wonderful thing.

How do you remove the natural urge we all have to talk yourself out of taking that bold step your heart is telling you to take? According to Mel Robbins, author of *The 5 Second Rule*, procrastination is not a character flaw. It is a natural reaction. It is fear. It is built into your brain.

"Feeling fear is natural. Listening to it is a choice." – Mel Robbins

You can get caught in or get past procrastination, Robbins says. And you've got five seconds to make your decision. She says in five seconds anyone can find the courage to make that move you know you need to make to improve your productivity, improve your health, or land the job of your dreams.

I believe her because the 5 Second Rule worked for me. Not long after I had written *The White Shirt* and published this book on my own, a friend of mine recommended that I contact a book agent that he knew. I definitely wanted an agent and publisher, but I kept putting off making contact because I was afraid of rejection.

Then one day I started listening to an audio version of Robbins's book, *The 5 Second Rule*. And I decided to act. I composed an email message to the potential agent, counted down 5-4-3-2-1 and pushed send. In about 10 minutes I got an email back from the agent asking, "When can we talk?" We talked that day. By the end of that same week, I received a contract to sign from a publisher in New York.

The 5 Second Rule is a modern proven strategy that builds on the "Ready, Set, Go" practice Cyrus learned from his father. As we all know, it's much easier to roll over and sleep for a few more minutes. The problem is, you just might miss the best part of your life. On the other hand, when you take that first action, you'll feel like doing more.

If you are serious about overcoming the procrastination hurdle, go right now to www.melrobbins.com and learn about *The 5 Second Rule: Change Your Life in 5 Seconds.*

AND NOW:
HOW DO I FIND IT?

Congratulations! Your journey to designing your career strategy is complete. Now it's time to work your plan and pursue your strategy. Meet with your dialogue partner once every week, or whatever schedule fits both of you. When you meet, discuss your progress and share notes from your journal. Use these blank pages to continue your notes.

On the website you'll find additional resources, ideas, and tools to support your success during this phase.

Plans fail for lack of counsel, but with many advisers they succeed.

—Proverbs 15:22 (NIV)

The White Shirt Book website is whiteshirtbook.com

ACKNOWLEDGMENTS

My deepest gratitude goes to all of my colleagues and friends who contributed to this little book of mine. However, knowing me as I do, I have most likely missed a few of you. If the one I missed is you, please forgive my recurring brain stones episodes. Remember, "It's not you. It's me."

Many thanks to...

Constance Tate, my mother, who is my Lena, my constant encourager and prayer warrior.

Patricia Tate, my wife and other prayer warrior. She shared her gifts of detailing and knowing the soul of a story and courageously suggested the little adjustments that made this book's voice ring clearer.

Bradley, my son, for his steadfast support and grace-filled critiques and his son, my grandson, Jakob, a wise-beyond-his-years teenager, who made the final correct call on the front cover design.

Norman Jetmundsen, Jr., a dear friend, fellow author and the one who opened the door for me to meet Bruce Barbour.

Bruce Barbour, my agent, who took a risk on an unknown writer and pushed my book in front of David Hancock, founder and CEO of Morgan James Publishing, who saw something in this book as well.

Minnie Lamberth, my copywriter and friend, who applied her amazing craft to mold my vision and ideas into a storyline and happily took care of many publishing details above and beyond my initial request and her originally assigned mission.

Gayle Christopher for sharing her gifts in innovative website design and steady voice in marketing.

David Lamb, my public relations coach and resource connecter plus being my voiceover guy.

Suzanne Davis who reviewed the manuscript through her seasoned theological eyes.

Rabbi Jonathan Miller for his acceptingly joyful approach to everything and his sage advice on character names and context.

My few raving fans and unrelenting friends who graciously offered endorsements and gave time out of their busy lives to help push my book out there: Elizabeth Jeffries, Julie Young, Tom Stackhouse, Lezlee Freeman, Pete and Gloria Russell, Robert Russell, Shan Gill, Meghan Stallworth, and all the members of the Sunrise Rotary Club of Birmingham.

ABOUT THE AUTHOR

Michael Alan Tate is founder and president of On the Same Page Consulting, a management consulting firm that provides strategic facilitation for executive teams and career coaching for individuals facing significant work/life transitions. *The White Shirt* is based on the simple principles and straightforward strategies that have worked for his clients for over twenty years. Mike is also the author of *Design a Life That Works*, a book for successful people who want to get their career, family, and faith on the same page. He writes a monthly blog, The Leadership and Life Journal. Mike's website is www.michaelalantate.com.

MICHAEL ALAN TATE
Author & President of On the Same Page Consulting, Inc.

Successful leaders facing significant changes rely on Michael Alan "Mike" Tate for handcrafted strategies to experience a healthy transition in their leadership and life. This author is also a popular speaker and retreat facilitator on designing an On the Same Page Plan© for your career, your team or your organization in less time that you ever imagined.

As an executive coach, consultant and strategist for more than twenty years, Mike's experiences have made it clear that busy people want to make good decisions faster, have fun doing it, and see something happen sooner than later. As he often says, "A darn good plan today is better that an perfect plan six months from tomorrow."

Visit his websites to see some samples of his On the Same Page plans, learn about his unique consulting approach, and take a peak at his books: *Design a Life that Works*, *The White Shirt*, and *On the Same Page*. You can also sign up for his monthly newsletter the *Leadership and Life Journal* at:

www.michaelalantate.com

designalifebook.com

whiteshirtbook.com

Sharpen your Focus… Strengthen Relationships… Simplify Everything

Morgan James
Speakers Group

We connect Morgan James published
authors with live and online events
and audiences who will benefit
from their expertise.

Morgan James makes all of our titles available
through the Library for All Charity Organization.

www.LibraryForAll.org